A
STRAIGHTFORWARD
GUIDE
TO

PRODUCING YOUR OWN WILL

Philip Kingsley

British cataloguing in Publication Data. A catalogue record is available for this book from the British library.

978-1-84716-786-6

Printed by 4edge Ltd www.4edge.co.uk
Cover design by Bookworks Islington

CONTENTS

Introduction

4

Glossary of terms

Useful Addresses

Appendix 1-Example of Administration accounts

Appendix 2-sample letters to send when dealing with wills and probate

Appendix 3-Sample forms used in probate

*****

Introduction

Over thirty million adults in the UK do not make a will. More worrying still, 76% of people with dependant children have not made a will, nor have 80% of couples living together without marrying. Yet those who die intestate can leave behind confusion and heartache because they have failed to make provisions for their loved ones. For example, if both parents die at the same time, in a car crash or similar accident, custody of their children may not go to the person they intended unless their wishes are made clear in a will.

Common misconceptions

A large percentage of people wrongly believe that if they die without making a will their husband or wife will inherit all their assets automatically. Similarly, almost 90% of parents who are married or in civil partnerships are unaware that if they die without a will the surviving partner will inherit a maximum of £250,000 from the state. Half the remainder of the estate would go directly to the children while the surviving partner would receive a life interest in the other half which would pass to the children on the surviving partner's death.

This brief book is intended, mainly, for the person who wishes to understand the law and practice of drawing up an effective will and also the law as it affects probate and also the steps towards obtaining probate. It will also be very useful for those who are using a solicitor but wish to know more about the processes behind drawing up and executing a will.

There are more and more companies appearing on the scene now which will handle your will for you and also the process of probate but who will also charge hefty fees for the privilege. They will also charge you an annual fee for storing the will and can make costly mistakes which cause stress and loss for those dealing with the estate of the deceased. Unregulated will writers are operating without insurance or training, primarily because at the moment there is no regulation surrounding will writing and anyone is able to write a will. One of the major risks is that will-writing firms often ensure that they have themselves appointed as a sole of joint executor-the person responsible for administering the estate when the customer dies, then charge way over the odds to the bereaved relatives. Therefore you should avoid will writing firms, in fact avoid anyone other than a qualified solicitor. Banks have also been getting into the act often charging extortionate fees for the privilege. However, in 2011, Barclays, Lloyds, HSBC and the RBS group all voluntarily agreed to review their will writing practices.

In many cases, people can write up their own wills and also apply for and handle the process of probate, choosing to get the help of a solicitor as and when needed. For anyone with a complicated estate, which is increasingly likely with today's changing family life, it is advisable to use a qualified solicitor to assist you with a will or handle probate.

Finally, there is another area of unregulated work, that of tracing heirs to an estate which has become another big industry which is leading to problems for those beneficiaries in that they have to pay big fees when located. This has been highlighted on the BBC2 series, *Heir*

Hunters. We will discuss the process of probate at the end of the book. Again the advice is to employ a qualified solicitor and avoid any outside interference, ensuring that the solicitors are not using expensive companies to track down beneficiaries..

****

Chapter 1

Producing a Will-Key Points

The main principle underlying any will is that, if you have possessions, or any other assets, then you need to organise a will that will ensure that chosen people benefit after your death.

In the majority of cases, a person's affairs are relatively uncomplicated and should not involve the use of a solicitor.

There are certain basic rules to be followed in the formation of a will and if they are then it should be legally binding.

The only inhibiting factor on the disposal of your assets will be any tax liability following death, which will be dealt with later in this book. There are a number of other factors to consider, however:

• Age of person making a will

A will made by anyone under the age of eighteen, known as a minor, will not be valid unless that person is a member of the services (armed forces) and is on active service.

• Mental health considerations

A will formed by a person, who was insane at the time of writing, will not be valid. Mental illness in itself is not a barrier to creating a will, as long as proof can be shown that the person was not insane at the time of writing. Subsequent mental illness, following the formation of a will, will not be a barrier to a will's validity.

Definition of insanity

Insanity, or this particular condition, will normally apply to anyone certified as such and detained in a mental institution. In addition, the Mental Health Act covers those in " a state of arrested or incomplete development of mind which includes sub-normality of intelligence and is of such a nature or degree that the patient is incapable of living an independent life or guarding against serious exploitation.

In any situation where there is doubt as to a persons capabilities then it is always best to have any will validated by an expert. This applies to anyone, not just those classified as insane.

The main point of any will is that, in the final analysis, a court would have to be satisfied that the contents of the will are genuine, there has not been any attempt whatsoever to alter the contents or to influence that persons mind. The person writing the will must have fashioned its contents with no outside interference.

Unfortunately, the history of the production of people's last will and testament is littered with greedy and unscrupulous persons who wish to gain from another's demise. It is necessary to be careful!

The Main Reasons for Making a Will

The main reason for making a will is to ensure that you make the choice as to who you leave your possessions to, and not the state. You can also impose any specific conditions you want in your will. For example, you can impose age conditions or conditions relating to the need to perform certain duties before benefiting.

If you do not make a will, or your will is invalid then, on your death, the law of intestacy will apply to the disposal of your estate. You will have had no say and certain criteria are applied by the state, which will take responsibility.

In the circumstances described above, after costs such as funeral and administration of other aspects of death, an order of preference is established.

The law of intestacy

If a person dies without leaving a will or without leaving a valid will, the laws of intestacy apply. It is important to note that the Inheritance and Trustees Power Act 2014 has introduced changes regarding who will inherit under an intestate estate and also how much they inherit. The changes will have no effect on people who die with assets worth less than £250,000.

The law of intestacy rests on the question of: who survived the deceased?

If there is a lawful spouse or civil partner and the deceased died **leaving children** then the spouse receives the first £250,000 in respect of assets solely in the deceased's name plus half of the remaining capital.

Children receive half remaining capital, then on the death of the spouse/civil partner the children receive the remaining capital.

If there is a lawful spouse/civil partner and the deceased died **leaving no children**, the spouse receives the entire estate. This is a new provision introduced following the introduction of the above mentioned Inheritance and Trustees Powers Act 2014, which came into force in October 2014. the changes apply in England and Wales.

If there are children, but no spouse or civil partner, everything goes to the children in equal shares.

If there are parent(s) but no spouse or civil partner or children then everything goes to parents in equal shares.

If there are brothers or sisters, but no spouse or civil partner, or children or parents everything goes to brothers and sisters of the whole blood equally.

If there are no brothers or sisters of the whole blood, then all goes to brothers and sisters of the half blood equally.

If there are grandparents, but no spouse or civil partner, or children or parents, or brothers and sisters everything goes to the grandparents equally.

If there are uncles and aunts, but no spouse or civil partner, or children or parents, or brothers or sisters or grandparents, then everything goes to uncles and aunts of the whole blood equally.

If there are no uncles and aunts of the whole blood, then all goes to uncles and aunts of the half blood equally.

If there is no spouse or civil partner and no relatives in any of the categories shown above then everything goes to the Crown.

A spouse is a person who was legally married to the deceased when he or she died. A civil partner is someone who was in a registered civil partnership with the deceased when he or she died. It doesn't include people simply living together as unmarried partners or as common law husband and wife.

The term children includes children born in or out of wedlock and legally adopted children; it also includes adult sons and daughters. It does not, however, include stepchildren.

Brothers and sisters of the whole blood have the same mother and father. Brothers and sisters of the half blood (more commonly referred to as half brothers and sisters) have just one parent in common.

Uncles and aunts of the whole blood are brothers and sisters of the whole blood of the deceased's father or mother.

Uncles and aunts of the half blood are brothers and sisters of the half blood of the deceased's father or mother.

It is important to note that if any of the deceased children die before him, and leave children of their own (that is grandchildren of the deceased) then those grandchildren between them take the share that their mother or father would have taken if he or she had been alive. This also applies to brothers and sisters and uncles and aunts of the deceased who have children – if any of them dies before the deceased, the share that he or she would have had if he or she were still alive, goes to his or her children between them.

The principle applies through successive generations – for example a great grandchild will take a share of the estate if his father and his grandfather (who were respectively the grandson and son of the deceased) both died before the deceased.

It is important to note that if any of the following situations apply to you, or if you are in any doubt whatsoever, you should seek legal advice before distributing the estate of a person who has died without leaving a will:

- The deceased died before 4th of April 1988
- Anyone entitled to a share of the estate is under 18
- Someone died before the deceased and the share he or she would have had goes to his or her children instead
- The spouse/civil partner dies within 28 days of the deceased.

A spouse or civil partner must outlive the deceased by 28 days before they become entitled to any share of the estate.

An ex-wife or civil partner (who was legally divorced from the deceased or whose civil partnership with the deceased was dissolved before the date of death) gets nothing from the estate under the rules of intestacy, but he/she may be able to make a claim under the inheritance (Provision for Family and Dependants) Act 1975, through the courts. Legal advice should be sought if making such a claim.

Anyone who is under 18 (except a spouse or civil partner of the deceased) does not get his or her share of the estate until he or she become 18, or marries under that age. It must be held on trust for him or her until he or she becomes 18 or gets married.

Apart from the spouse or civil partner of the deceased, only blood relatives, and those related by legal adoption, are entitled to share in the estate. Anyone else who is related through marriage and not by blood is not entitled to a share in the estate.

If anyone who is entitled to a share of the estate dies after the deceased but before the estate is distributed, his or her share forms part of his or her own estate and is distributed under the terms of his or her will or intestacy.

Great uncles and great aunts of the deceased (that is brothers and sisters of his or her grandparents) and their children are not entitled to a share in the estate.

Further changes under the Inheritance and Trustees Powers Act 2014

The definition of personal property/chattels has also changed. Under old rules, the term "chattels" was outdated and included old-fashioned terms such as "carriages", "linen" and "scientific instruments". Under new rules "personal chattels" includes all tangible moveable property, apart from property which consists of money or security for money, or property that was used solely or mainly for business purposes or was held solely as an investment

The old definition of chattels will still apply where a Will was executed before 1 October 2014 and makes reference to s55 (1) (x) (Administration of Estates Act 1925).

Under old rules, if an individual died leaving a child under the age of 18, who was subsequently adopted by someone else, there was a risk that the child may lose their inheritance from their natural parent. The new rules ensure that children will not lose any claim to inheritance if they were adopted after the death of a natural parent.

>****

Chapter 2

When to Produce a Will

It is essential that you make a will as soon as possible. If you leave it, there is a chance that you may never get round to doing it and may be reliant upon the state doing it for you. There is also the chance that you will leave a situation where people start to contest your possessions, fight amongst each other and fall out.

There are many things to consider when you decide to produce a will. As a person gets older, chances are that he or she will become wealthier. Savings grow, endowments increase, insurance policies become more valuable, property is purohased and so on. A bank balance in itself is no indioator of worth, as there are many other elements which add up to wealth.

Changes in personal circumstances often justify the need to make a will.

- Ownership of property
- Children
- Marriage or remarriage
- Employment

- Illness

- Divorce and separation

- Increase in personal wealth, such as an inheritance

Ownership of property

Ownership of property usually implies a mortgage. If you are wise it will also imply life insurance to at least the value of the property. It is very prudent to make a will which specifies exactly to whom the property will be left. As we have seen, the law of intestacy provides for the decision if you do not have a will.

Children

As we have seen, under the law of intestacy, any children you have will benefit after your death. However, it is very sensible, under a will, to specify how and when they will benefit. It could be that you may let someone else make that decision later on. Whatever, you should make it very clear in your will.

Marriage or remarriage

The most important point to remember is that marriage or remarriage will automatically revoke the provisions of any former will, although this is not the case in Scotland. Therefore, when marrying you should make certain that your will is up to date and that you have altered the provisions. In short, you should amend your will, or produce a new will in order to outline clearly what you want your new partner to have.

22

Employment

You should be very aware that certain types of employment carry greater risks than others. This will necessitate producing a will as soon as possible as if you are in a high-risk category then you need to ensure that those nearest you are catered for.

Illness

Illness is something that none of us want but cannot avoid if it decides to strike. No matter how healthy you are you should take this into account when considering putting together a will. In addition, some people have a family history of illness and chances are that they too could suffer. Therefore illness is a very real motivator for producing a will.

Divorce and separation

The law of intestacy states that if you die your divorced spouse/civil partner loses all rights to your estate. You may not want this to happen and make provisions in your will. Although children of any marriage will benefit It could be that you may wish to make slightly different provisions for different children.

Increase in personal wealth

Financial success, and inheritance will increase your wealth and inevitably make you estate more complicated. It is absolutely essential to ensure that you have a will and that you are updating that will regularly to take into account increased assets.

The provisions of a will

Having considered some of the many reasons for producing a will, it is now necessary to look at exactly what goes into a will.

Essentially, the purpose of a will is to ensure that everything you have accumulated in your life is disposed of in accordance with your own desires. The main areas to consider when formulating a will are:

- Money you have saved, in whatever form
- Any buildings (property) you have
- Any land you have
- Any insurance policies you have. This is of utmost importance
- Any shares you may own
- Trusts set up
- Any other personal effects

Money you have saved

Money is treated as part of your wider estate and will automatically go to those named as the main beneficiaries. However, you might wish to make individual bequests to other people outside your family. These have to be specified. When including any provisions in your will relating to money, you should be very clear about the whereabouts of any saving accounts or endowments, premium bonds etc. Life becomes very difficult if you have left sums of money but there is no knowledge of the whereabouts of this. Inevitably, solicitors have to be employed and this becomes very expensive indeed.

24

Property

It is necessary to make provisions for any property you have. If you are the sole owner of a property then you can dispose of it as you wish. Any organisation with a superior interest would take an interest, particularly if there are mortgages outstanding. It is important to remember that if you are a joint owner of a property, such as a joint tenancy, then on death this joint ownership reverts to the other joint owner, bringing it into sole ownership. Leasehold property can be different only in so much as the executor of an estate will usually need permission before assigning a lease. This can be obtained from the freeholder.

Land

Although the same principles apply to land as to property, indeed often the two are combined, in certain circumstances land may be owned separately. In this case the land and everything on it can be left in the will.

Insurance policies

The contents of any insurance policy needs to be checked carefully. In certain cases there are restrictions on who can benefit on death. Particular people may be specified and you have no alternative but to let such people benefit, even though your own circumstances may have changed. If there are no restrictions then you can bequeath any money as you see fit.

..

Shares and trusts

Shares can normally be bequeathed in a will as anything else. However, depending on the type of share, it is just possible that there may be restrictions. One such situation is where shares are held in a private company and there may be a buy back clause.

Trusts can be set up for the benefit of family and friends. However, a trust, by its very nature is complex as the law dealing with trusts is complex. It is absolutely essential, if you are considering setting up a trust to get specialist advice.

Personal effects

Although you are perfectly entitled to leave specific items of personal effects in your will, such legacies are separate from those of other possessions such as money or land. The law recognises that in some cases there may not be enough money to pay expenses related to your death. Any money owed will be retrieved from any financial gifts you have outlined. However, personal effects cannot be touched if you have clearly identified these in your will. This includes items of value such as jewelry. It is not enough to be general on this point. You must specify exactly what it is you are leaving and to whom. Remember, certain gifts will be taxable. We will be covering this later.

The funeral

It is common practice to include such matters as how you wish to be buried, in what manner and the nature of the ceremony, in your will. You should discuss these arrangements with your next of kin in addition to specifying them in your will as arrangements may be made for a funeral before details of a will are made public. Another way is to detail your wishes in a letter and pass this on to your executor to ensure that the details are known beforehand.

There is no reason why any of your instructions should not be carried out, subject to the law. However, your executor can override your wishes if necessary and expedient.

You can, in addition, make known your wishes for maintenance of your grave after your death. Agreement of the local authority, or relevant burial authority must be sought and there is no obligation on them to do this. In addition, there is a time limit of 99 years in force.

The use of your body after death

It could be that you have decided to leave your body for medical research or donate your organs. This can be done during your final illness, in writing or in front of a minimum of two witnesses. You should contact your local hospital or General Practitioner about this, they will supply you with more details.

Making a recital

A recital consists of a statement at the end of your will which explains how and why you have drawn up a will in the way you have. This is not commonly done but sometimes may be necessary, especially if you have cut people out of your will but do not intend to cause confusion or hurt. Recitals are sometimes necessary in order to clarify a transfer of authority to others on your death. This could be in business for example. In addition, you may wish to recognise someone's contribution to your life, for example a long serving employee or a particular friend.

*****

Chapter 3

Making Provisions in a Will

Who to name

When including persons, or organisations, in your will it is better to form a separate list right at the outset.

Naming individuals in your will

There are certain criteria which apply when naming individuals in a will, although in principle you can name who you want. Any person considered an adult, i.e. over 18, can benefit from your will. However, if a person cannot be traced within a time period of seven years after being named, or dies before you, then the amount left in your will to that person is included in what is known as the residue of your estate, what is left after all bequests. You can also make a bequest in your will to cover that eventuality, that is for another named person to benefit in his or her place.

If the bequest is to your own children or any other direct descendant and they die before you then the gift will automatically go to their children, unless there is something to the contrary in your will. In addition, if you make a gift to two or more people and one dies then that share is automatically passed to the other (joint owner).

Children

You are entitled to leave what you want in your will to children whether they are illegitimate or stepchildren. Stepchildren should be stipulated in your will. If children are under 18 then it will be probably necessary to leave property such as land, in trust for them until they reach 18 or any other age stated in the will. No child under 18 can be a trustee.

Those people who are not British citizens, i.e. foreigners can benefit from your will in the same way as anyone else. The only real restriction to this is if there is a state of war between your own country and theirs, in which case it will be necessary to wait until peace is declared.

Mental illness

There is nothing currently in law which prevents a person suffering mental illness from receiving a bequest under a will. Obviously, depending on the state of mind of that person it could be that someone may have to accept the gift and take care of it on the person's behalf.

Bankruptcy

If a person is either bankrupt or facing bankruptcy then if that person receives a gift there is a chance that it could end up in the hands of a creditor.

To avoid this happening you can establish a protective trust which will enable the person in receipt of the gift to enjoy any interest arising from the gift during a specific time.

30

Animals

It is possible to leave money to animals for their care and well-being. There is a time limit involved for receipt of the money, which is currently a period of 21 years.

Groups

There is no problem legally with leaving money and other gifts to groups or organisations. However, it is necessary to ensure that the wording of the will is structured in a certain way. It is necessary to understand some of the legislation concerning charities, in order that your bequest can be deemed charitable.

Leaving money/gifts to charities

Many people leave bequests to charity. Major charities often give advice to individuals and other organisations on how to do that. Smaller charities can pose a problem as they may not be as sound and as well administered as larger ones. It is best to stipulate an alternative charity in the event of the smaller one ceasing to operate. If for whatever reason your bequest cannot be passed on to the group concerned then it will be left in the residue of your estate and could be liable to tax. There are a number of causes which might be deemed as charitable. These are:

• Educational causes
• Help for the community
• Animal welfare
• Help for the elderly

- Disabled
- Religious groups
- Sick, such as hospices

In the event of making a bequest to a charitable cause, it is certain that you will need expert advice, as with the setting up of trusts. You should also read chapter 6, The Role of the Courts, in a case where a person who left money to animal charities had her will successfully challenged.

>****

Chapter 4

The Correct Form of a Will

The writing of a will and the way you word it, is of the utmost importance and it is here that skill is needed. If you word the will wrongly then it can be contested, rejected and your estate could be administered by the state.

As long as you observe certain rules then there is no reason why you should go wrong, however.

One of the key rules is that there should be nothing in your will that can be ambiguous or open to interpretation. It is essential to ensure that your intentions are crystal clear. It will probably be necessary to get someone else to look at your will to ensure that it is understood by others.

Preparation of will

A will can of course be rewritten. However, it is very important indeed to ensure that you have spent enough time in the initial preparation stages of your will as it could be enacted at any time, in the event of sudden death. If your possessions are numerous then it is highly likely that the preparation stage will be fairly lengthy as the dividing up will take more thought. This gets more complicated depending on your other circumstances, such as whether you are married or single, have children, intend to leave money to organizations, etc.

You need to make a clear list of what it is you have in order to be able to achieve clarity in your will. For example, property and other possessions will take in any buildings and land you own plus money in various accounts or other forms of saving. In addition there could be jewelry and other valuables to take into account. It is necessary to quantify the current value of these possessions. It is also necessary to balance this out by making a list of any outstanding loans/mortgages or other debts you may have. Funeral costs should come into this. It is essential that you do not attempt to give away more than you actually have and also to deduce any tax liabilities from the final amount after debts. The wording of any will is always done with tax liability in mind.

Listing those who will benefit from your will

Making a list of beneficiaries is obviously necessary, including all groups, individuals and others who will benefit. With each beneficiary you should list exactly what it is that you bequeath. If a trust is necessary, then note this and note down the name of proposed trustees. These persons should be in agreement before being named. Contact any charities that will benefit. They can supply you with a legacy clause to include in your will.

The most important point, at this stage, is that you ensure that what you are leaving does not exceed the estate and that, if liable for tax, then there is sufficient left over to meet these liabilities.

34

.   Make a note of any recitals that you wish to include in your will and exactly what you wish to say.

The choice of an executor of your will

The job of any executor is to ensure that your will is administered in accordance with the terms therein as far as is legally possible at that time. It is absolutely essential to ask those people is they consent to being an executor. They may well refuse which could pose problems. You can ask friends or family or alternatively you can ask a solicitor or your bank. They will make a charge for this. However, they are much less likely to make a mistake in the execution of the will than an untrained individual. They will charge and this should be provided for.

If you do choose to appoint an untrained executor, then it is good policy to appoint at least two in order to ensure that there is an element of double-checking and that there are enough people to fulfill the required duties.

Power of attorney

You may want to consider giving someone the power of attorney to handle your affairs. A power of attorney simply gives a person the power to act for somebody else in their financial affairs or in health and personal welfare. (Rules in Scotland are different). If you are away or fall ill, you will need someone to look after your affairs - and that requires a power of attorney. (If this happens and you had not given a power of attorney, your friends and relatives would have to go to court, which would take time and cost money)

Ending the power

When you have given a power of attorney, there are two ways in which it can be ended. You can end it yourself by using a deed of revocation or it will end automatically if you, the donor, lose 'mental capacity.' This is where problems can arise. Suppose you gave your partner an ordinary power of attorney to handle your bank account while you go on your overseas business trip; you are mugged while on your trip and lie unconscious in hospital. Your power of attorney is ended because you are mentally out of action; for the same reason you cannot give a new power of attorney.

Your partner cannot legally access your bank account or have any involvement in your affairs: catch 22? Until last year, the answer to this puzzle was to create an Enduring Power of Attorney. Under an EPA when you were mugged on your overseas trip, your partner and/or solicitor would register with the court and they could then act on your behalf.

New EPAs cannot be created since October 2007 though any existing EPAs can be registered when that becomes necessary.

New lasting powers

EPA's have been replaced by Lasting Powers of Attorney which have separate sections for personal welfare and for property and affairs. Each of these has to be registered separately and the LPA can only be used - similar to an EPA - once it has been registered with the Office of the Public Guardian. If you want to change your mind, you can cancel all the different Powers of Attorney, so long as you are still mentally

36

capable. This may all sound elaborate but it represents the only answer to the situation where you cannot manage your affairs because of accident, illness, age or whatever - but someone needs to do so.

The need for a power of attorney is now that much greater because banks and financial institutions are more aware of their legal responsibilities. Formerly, a friendly bank manager might have been prepared to help your partner sort out what needed to be done while you were out of action. Now, your friendly bank manager is more likely to stick to the legal rules, if only to protect himself and his employer.

The presentation of your will

You can either prepare your will on ordinary sheets of paper or used specially prepared forms which can be obtained from stationers or book shops. Bookshops will usually sell "will packs" which take you through the whole preparation stage, from contemplation to completion. Try to avoid handwriting your will. If it cannot be read then it will be invalid. You should always try to produce it on a word processor or typewriter. This can be more easily altered at any time.

The advantage of using a pre-printed form is that it has all of the required phrases on it and you just fill in the blanks. It just may be that you are not in the position to write your will, as you may be one of the considerable numbers of people who cannot read or write in this country. In this case, you can get someone else to write it for you although it is essential that you understand the contents. Get someone else, independent of the person who wrote it to read it back to you to ensure that the contents reflect your wishes.

The Wording of a will

The wording of a will is of the utmost importance as it is absolutely necessary to ensure that you produce a clear document which is an instrument of your own will. The following are some words, which appear in wills, with an explanation of their precise meaning and pitfalls:

- o Beneficiary-this means someone or something that benefits as a result of a gift in a will.
- o Bequeath- "I bequeath" in a will usually refers to personal property such as personal property and money.
- o Children-this includes both legitimate and illegitimate children and also adopted children. Where a gift is to a child and that child has children and dies before the death of the person making the will then the gift will pass on to the child or children of that child if they are living at the time of the testators death unless an intention to the contrary appears in the will. "Children" does not usually include stepchildren and if you wish a stepchild to be included then this will need to be specified. Children will include stepchildren where there are only stepchildren alive at the time of making the will.

"Children" can also include grandchildren where it is clear that this was intended or there are only grandchildren and no other children are alive at the date of making a will. You should always specify grandchildren when you want them included.

- o Civil Partner-this means the person with whom the deceased has entered into a civil partnership with.

o Descendants-this means children, grandchildren, great grandchildren and so on down the line. A gift using this word is sometimes phrased "to my descendants living at my death" which includes all those who are alive at the time of the death of the person making a will. Male descendants means males who are descended from females as well as those who are descended from males. A gift to descendants means that they all take equal shares. If you wish each merely to take in default of a parent or parents (e.g. if a parent predeceases you) then add the words "per stirpes".

o Devise- "I devise" in a will usually refers to a gift of land, which includes a house.

o Executor/Executrix-this is the person or persons you appoint to administer your will and to carry out your wishes as expressed in your will. Anyone can be appointed an executor, usually expressed as a clause in your will. The few exceptions are those of a minor and those of unsound mind. Solicitors and banks can also be appointed.

Executors can also receive gifts under the will. The executor cannot charge fees, banks and solicitors do but the will must stipulate this. Because of the fact that executors can change their minds about taking on the task of administering your will, it is often better to have two.

o Family-this word should not be used if it can be helped as it has been interpreted in several different ways. It is, by and large, far to general.

o Husband/civil partner-this means the husband/civil partner at the time of making the will. In the event of a divorce, a person remains married until the decree absolute has been granted. Divorce alters the will in so far as any appointment of a former spouse as an executor becomes void, as do any bequests to that person, unless there is a contrary intention in the will.

Generally, if a marriage splits up it is best to review the provisions of a will.

o Infant-this means a child under the age of eighteen. Land is given to trustees (usually) if left to those under eighteen, as an infant cannot hold an estate in land.

o Issue-this means all descendants but has been interpreted as having several meanings. In a simple will its use should be avoided altogether as again, it is far too general.

o Minor-this has the same meaning as infant.

o Nephews-the meaning of this term depends upon the context of the will. It is far safer, in any such general situation to be specific and name names.

o Next of kin-this means the closest blood relation.

o Nieces-the same applies as for nephews.

o Pecuniary legacy-this means a gift of money in a will.

o Residue-this means the amount that is left of your estate after effect has been given to all the gifts in your will and testamentary and other expenses have been paid.

o Survivor-this may apply to persons who are not born at the time of the will. Therefore, a gift to all those who survive a person leaving the will could include all brothers and sisters not yet born.

o Testamentary expenses-in a will the residue of an estate may be left to a person after all expenses. This includes all known expenses, such as the costs of administering the will.

o Trustee-a trustee is someone entrusted to look after property for another until a certain age is attained or condition fulfilled. There should always be more than one trustee with two being a usual number.

o Wife-this means the wife at the time of making the will. Again, in the event of a divorce, then the decree absolute must be granted before that person ceases to be a wife.

Safekeeping of a will

A will must always be kept safe and should be able to be located at the time of your death. You may spend a great deal of time on your will. However, if it cannot be found then it will be assumed that you have not made one. It is best practice to deposit the will with your or your family solicitor.

*****

Chapter 5

The Contents of The Will

When writing a will, there is a recognised format which must be followed for the will to be deemed legal.

The following content constitutes the basic outline:

- A will states that this is your last will and testament
- Your full name and address must be on the will and the date of the will
- All previous wills, if they exist, must be revoked in writing
- There must be an appointment and payment of executors
- Provision for the appointment of a firm of solicitors, if appropriate
- The method of disposal of your body, whether by cremation or burial or whether you have chosen to leave your body for medical purposes. This is not essential
- Payment of testamentary expenses
- Payment of inheritance tax if you are giving gifts free of tax
- Any recital, e.g. any statement of affection or other which you wish to pass
- A list of specific items to be left in your will

- A list of all pecuniary legacies, headed "I give and bequeath the following pecuniary legacies"
- A list of all gifts of land headed "I give and devise"
- A clause dealing with the residue of your estate, such as any property and money remaining after all the gifts and payments of expenses in your will have been made
- Your usual signature
- The signature of two witnesses, neither of whom or whose spouses are given any gift in the will. There should be a statement that they were both present at the same time and either saw you making your signature or acknowledging that the signature is yours.

Making a list of the key steps to be taken when preparing a will

It is essential, before beginning to draft out your will to follow a check-list of the key steps to be taken:

- Make a complete list of all property that you own, including any future property. Deduct any mortgages or loans in order to arrive at a figure which can be left in your will, or a net worth
- Next, make a list of all those people who will benefit under your will (beneficiaries)
- Note any expressions of affection that you want to make in your will
- Organise your executors. As we have seen, these can be members of your family, a bank, solicitor etc. You need to know the fees involved if you are using a professional practice.

- These should be allowed for in the will. Likewise, you may wish to leave something to those who act as executors for you

- Prepare your will, preferably typewritten on quality paper

- Make a list of all bequests of your goods that you wish to leave and a list of all the legacies of the money that you wish to leave

- Think about any specific beneficiaries and what this involves, such as a charity. Do you need to contact them and ask for their number or to enlist any help that they may give? Likewise, you may want to leave money to a pet. You will probably need advice on this

- Consider whether you want to create any trusts. Again, you will need advice concerning these

- Make sure that witnesses have signed your will

- Ensure that your signature is your usual one

- Make sure that the will is dated the day that it is signed.

- Fold up your will, place into an envelope and mark it "The last will and testament of_____ (add your name)

- Put your will in a safe place and tell your executors and next of kin where it is kept

- Remember to alter your will as your circumstances change. Destroy any old copies of wills.

The Thirty-day clause

If your immediate beneficiary dies within days of your own demise, unlikely but not unknown, the situation may well arise where the gifts left by you will pass elsewhere. To prevent this happening, you can

44

make provision in your will stipulating another beneficiary should the immediate beneficiary not survive you by thirty days.

The use of a statutory will form

Statutory will forms are very helpful in that they have the necessary forms of words, in many cases. There are a number of forms. Form 2 for example, allows you to give all your possessions to someone without having to identify each possession. There are a number of other forms catering for different situations. One such form is form 4 which is designed for charitable bequests.

International wills

A provision now exists which is designed to aid those people who have property in a number of different countries. They can now make one will and have it administered in any country which is party to the convention. This can be done regardless of where the will was drawn up or where the assets are. There are a certain number of criteria to be followed, however:

- The will must be in writing. It can be in any language
- The person whose will it is must declare in front of a solicitor/notary that the will is really his or hers and this must be witnessed by two people
- The person making the will must then sign it at the end, and sign and number each page, in the presence of a solicitor and witnesses who must sign at the end. The date must be added by a solicitor,

45

and a certificate must be attached, which should include details of where the will is kept.

It will be necessary to seek advice regarding international wills as they have only relatively recently been introduced.

See below for sample last will and testament.

Sample Last Will and Testament

This is the last Will and Testament

Of me_____ of (address)_____

Made this_____ day of_____

1. I hereby revoke all former wills and testamentary dispositions heretofore made by me.

2. I appoint (executors and trustees) (hereinafter called "my trustees" which expression where the context admits includes any trustee or trustees hereof for the time being whether original or substituted) to be the executors and trustees thereof and I declare that any of my trustees being a solicitor or other profession shall be entitled to charge accordingly.

3. I appoint_____

Of_____

To be the guardian after the death of my wife husband/civil partner_____ of any of my children who may then be minors.

4. If my wife or husband/civil partner survives me by thirty days (but not otherwise) I give to him or her absolutely (Subject to payment of debts and other expenses) all my estate both real and personal whatsoever and wheresoever not hereby or by any codicil hereto otherwise specifically disposed of.

1. If my wife or husband/civil partner as stated in this will is not living at my death the following provisions shall have effect:

I give all my estate both real and personal whatsoever and wheresoever not hereby or any codicil hereto otherwise specifically disposed of unto my trustees UPON TRUST to raise and discharge my debts and funeral and testamentary expenses and all legacies given hereby or by any codicil hereto and any and all taxes payable by reason of my death in respect of property given free of tax and subject thereto UPON TRUST to pay and divide the same equally between my children

_____Name

_____Address

And_____Of

_____

as shall survive me and attain the age of 18 years provided always that if any child of mine shall die before reaching 18 yrs or marry under that age leaving a child or children such last such last mentioned child or children shall take by substitution and if more than one in equal shares the share of my estate which his or her or their parent would have taken if he or she had survived me.

2.   If neither my wife/husband/civil partner nor children nor any of their issue are living at my death then I give all my estate, both real and personal whatsoever and wheresoever unto my trustees upon trust to raise and discharge thereout my debts and funeral and testamentary expenses and all legacies given hereby or by any codicil hereto and any and all taxes payable by reason of my death in respect of property given free of tax, and subject thereto UPON TRUST to pay and divide the same equally between:

_____Names

of_____Address

My Trustees shall have the following powers in addition to their general law powers:

a) to apply for the benefit of any beneficiary as my trustees think fit the whole or any part of the income from that part of my estate to which he is entitled or may in future be entitled.

b) to apply for the benefit of any beneficiary as my trustee thinks fit the whole or any part of the capital to which that beneficiary is entitled.

c) to exercise the power of appropriation conferred by section 41 of The Administration of Estates Act 1925 without obtaining any of the consents required by that section even though one or more of them may be beneficially interested.

d) to invest trust money and transpose Investment with the same full and unrestricted freedom in their choice of investments as if they were an absolute beneficial owner and to apply trust money at any time and from time to time in the purchase with vacant possession or in the improvement of any freehold or leasehold house and to permit the same to be used by any person or person having an interest or prospective Interest in my residuary estate upon such terms and conditions from time to time as my trustees in their absolute discretion may think fit.

e) To insure from loss or damage from fire or any other risk any property for the time being comprised in my residuary estate to any amount and even though a person is absolutely entitled to the property and to pay all premiums as due and any insurances out of the income or capital of my residuary estate.

I wish my body to be

Buried/cremated_____

In witness to this document I set my hand this _____day of_____

Signed by said witness_____Name

Signature_____

****

Chapter 6

The Role of the Courts

Courts have wide powers to make alterations to a persons will, after that person's death. It can exercise these powers if the will fails to achieve the intentions of the person who wrote it, as a result of a clerical error or a failure to understand the instructions of the person producing the will. In addition, if mental illness can be demonstrated at the time of producing the will then this can also lead to the courts intervening.

In 2015, a case was heard in the Court of Appeal which involved the daughter of Melita Jackson, Heather Ilott, challenging her mother's will on the grounds that it did not leave 'reasonable provision' for her in the will. Originally, Mrs. Jackson left the whole estate of £500,000 to animal charities. The Court of Appeal ruled in Mrs. Ilotts favour and awarded her £164,000 stating that she would otherwise face a life of poverty because she was on benefits and could not go on holiday or afford clothes for the children. the fact that Mrs Jackson had little connection to the charities she left the money to was a factor in the ruling.

What this ruling means is that wills can be challenged and the right of people to leave money and assets to who they want has been seriously challenged. The ruling has implications for how people need to draw up their wills and it is suggested that in future people would have to explain the reasons for why they left money to certain parties and demonstrate tangible connections to them.

In order to get the courts to exercise their powers, an application must be made within six months of the date on which probate is taken out. If gifts or other are distributed and a court order is made to rectify the will then all must be returned to be distributed in accordance with the court order.

If any part of a persons will appears to have no meaning or is ambiguous then the court will look at any surrounding evidence and the testators intention and will rectify the will in the light of this evidence.

The right to dispose of property

In general, the law allows an unfettered right to dispose of a persons property as they choose. However, as outlined above this can now be challenged. The right is also subject to tax and the courts powers to intervene. The law has been consolidated in the Inheritance (Provision for Family and Dependants Act) 1975. Certain categories of people can now apply to the court and be given money out of a deceased persons will. This can be done whether there is a will or not.

The husband or wife/civil partner of a deceased person can be given any amount of money as the court thinks reasonable. The 1975 Act implemented the recommendations of the Law Commission which felt that a surviving spouse should be given money out of an estate on the same principles as a spouse is given money when there is a divorce. This means that, even if a will is not made, or there are inadequate provisions then a surviving spouse can make an application to rectify the situation. The situation is different for other relations. They can apply to the court to have a will rectified but will receive far less than the spouse. The following can claim against a will:

- The wife or husband/civil partner of the deceased
- A former wife or former husband/civil partner of the deceased who has not remarried
- A child of the deceased
- Any person who is not included as a child of the deceased but who was treated by the deceased as a child of the family in relation to any marriage during his lifetime
- Any other person who was being maintained, even if only partly maintained, by the deceased just before his or her death

Former spouse/civil partner

There is one main condition under which a former spouse/civil partner can claim and that is that they have not remarried. In addition, such a claim would be for only essential maintenance which would stop on remarriage. There is one key exception, that is that if your death occurs within a year of divorce or legal separation, your former spouse can make a claim.

Child of the deceased

As the above, any claim by children can only be on the basis of hardship.

Stepchildren

This includes anyone treated as your own child and supported by you, including illegitimate children or those conceived before, but not born till after, your death. The claim can only cover essential maintenance.

Dependants

This covers a wide range of potential claimants. Maintenance only is payable. There needs to be evidence of full or partial maintenance prior to death. Such support does not have to be financial, however.

There is another situation where the court can change a will after your death. This relates directly to conditions that you may have imposed on a beneficiary in order to receive a gift which are unreasonable. If the court decides that this is the case, that particular condition becomes void and does not have to be fulfilled.

If the condition involved something being done before the beneficiary receives the gift then the beneficiary does not receive the gift. If the condition involved something being done after the beneficiary received the gift then the beneficiary can have the gift without condition. If the beneficiary does not receive the gift, as in the above, then either the will can make alternative provision or the gift can form part of the residue of the estate.

Unreasonable conditions can be many, one such being any condition that provides reason or incentive to break up a marriage, intention to remain celibate or not to remarry or one that separates children.

54

There are others which impinge on religion, general behaviour and crime. An unreasonable condition very much depends on the perception of the beneficiary and the perception of the courts.

A beneficiary can lose the right to a bequest, apart from any failure to meet conditions attached to a bequest. Again, a court will decide in what circumstance this is appropriate. Crime could be a reason, such as murder, or evidence of coercion or harassment of another person in pursuit of selfish gain.

****

Chapter 7

Wills and Taxation

The formation of a will which enables you to minimise your tax liability is of the utmost importance. It is likely, if you are well off that you will want to consult a solicitor or financial advisor in order to gain the appropriate advice. It could be that you own a house which over the years has appreciated considerably which has resulted in the property being worth a considerable amount. This may mean that you could be liable for inheritance tax.

A book of this length cannot possibly give you in depth advice concerning your tax situation. However, what it can do is outline the current rules relating to tax and wills generally. It is very important to ensure that your will is updated regularly in order to keep abreast of the changing tax laws. The wealthier that you become the more important this becomes.

Deed of variation

Any change to a legal document is, in the main, achieved through a deed of variation. Within two years of a death, a beneficiary of a will may alter that deed in writing. For the purposes of inheritance tax the changed will is regarded as having been made by the dead person and substituted for that provision in the will or under the rules of intestacy.

Tax will only be payable under the new provision. This is still true even if the beneficiary received the property and makes a gift of it or disclaims a legacy within two years of the death. The law governing this is set out in s. 142 Inheritance Tax Act 1984. In order to comply with s142 the disclaimer must be in writing, refer specifically to the provision in the will and be signed by the person making the change.

The deed should be sent as soon as possible to the Capital Taxes Office. Where a person redirects property or makes a gift of it within the two-year period he/she must give notice (written) to the Capital Taxes Office within six months of doing it that he wants this provision to apply. If the effect is to increase the liability to inheritance tax, then the executors must join in the notice and can refuse on the ground that they do not have sufficient assets in the estate to pay the extra tax.

Inheritance tax

Inheritance tax was introduced under the 1986 Finance Act to replace Capital Transfer Tax. It is a tax on what is known as "transfer of value" meaning transfer under the terms of a will, or the rules of intestacy which reduce an estate. The amount which is liable to tax is the amount less any exemptions which are detailed further on. For tax purposes, the amount of the estate is the valuation of the estate of the dead person immediately before death. The tax is levied on transfers made by the dead person on death or *within seven years of death.*

Amount of inheritance tax payable

This is dependant on three factors:

- The value of the estate
- The value of any substantial gifts made within the last seven years
- Any exemptions from inheritance tax on ones death such as those on gifts to a surviving spouse, charities etc.

If a person is resident (domiciled) in the United Kingdom the tax applies to all that person property wherever it may be situated at home or abroad. If a person is domiciled abroad then the tax is applicable only to property in the United Kingdom.

The threshold for inheritance tax is 40% on the estate after exempt transfers and after the current tax threshold of £325,000 (2018/19) (check current provisions with your tax office). The amount is increased (usually) each year from 6th April in line with the increase in the Retail Price Index for the year to the previous December. However, the Chancellor announced, in the July 2015 budget, that he was increasing the IHT allowance to £1m (for a couple) for the family home. People will not have to pay IHT on properties worth less than £1million. This will be phased in from April 2017. However, there are a few things to note. The 'Family Homes Allowance' will apply only to property left to direct descendants, children, grandchildren, great grandchildren and so on. Stepchildren will also count.

The allowance will not apply to indirect descendants such as nieces and nephews. It is also suggested that advice should be sought when thinking of downsizing as the new IHT rules may affect your tax liabilities.

Exemptions from tax

The following are exempt for the purposes of inheritance tax liability:

- All gifts between the dead person and spouse. If the dead person is domiciled in the United Kingdom, and the husband/wife is not then the exemption is limited to £55,000.
- Lifetime gifts which represent normal expenditure out of the dead persons income during their life. Where payments are made by the dead person which did not change the dead persons standard of living then such amounts if paid seven years prior to the death will not be included in the estate.
- Lifetime gifts not exceeding £3000 in any one tax year. A person can make gifts totaling not more than £3000 in any year irrespective of the number of people to whom the amounts are given, otherwise any amounts over this will be included in the value of the estate if the person dies within seven years.
- Gifts in any one tax year to a maximum of £250 per person. There is no limit on the number of people to whom such gifts can be given so long as each one does not exceed £250 in any one tax year. These amounts are additional to the £3000 mentioned above but only to the extent that the total to any one individual in any tax year does not exceed £250.
- Gifts in consideration of marriage. Wedding gifts by a parent to his or her child are exempt by up to £5000, by a grandparent or other more distant relative up to £2500 and by other people up to £1000. This applies to each parent or grandparent.

- Lifetime gifts for the maintenance of a spouse or former spouse/civil partner, children and dependant relatives. In respect of a child, the exemption is to the age of 18 or completion of full time education if later. This is available for stepchildren and adopted children, plus illegitimate children. The child must be of the donor or his or her spouse.

- All gifts to charities

- Gifts to political parties unless they are made within the year of the date of the death, in which case up to £100,000 is exempt, but any amount above that will be included in the value of the estate.

- Gifts to organisations which deal with preservation of the national heritage or of a public nature such as the British Museum. This category includes gifts to most museums and art galleries.

- Certain types of properties are exempt, including agricultural land, business property, historic houses and woodlands plus works of art.

Business property

Since 1992 there has been 100% relief for the following categories of business property:

- Sole proprietor or partner

- Life tenants business or interest in a business

- A holding of shares or securities which by itself, or in conjunction with other holdings owned by the transferor gives control of the company (whether quoted or unquoted) Unquoted shares which by themselves or in conjunction with other shares or securities owned by the transferor give control of more than 25% of the votes.

- There is 50% relief for the following:
- Shares in a company which do not qualify under 3 above and which are not quoted on a recognised stock exchange.
- Land, buildings, plant or machinery owned by a partner or controlling shareholder and used wholly or mainly in the business of the partnership or company immediately before the transfer, provided that the partnership interest or shareholding would itself, if it were transferred, qualify for business relief.
- Any land or building, plant or machinery which, immediately before the transfer was used wholly for the purposes of a business carried on by the transferor, was settled property in which he or she was then beneficially entitled to an interest in possession and was transferred while the business itself was being retained.

Potentially Exempt Transfers

Any gift outside the exemptions mentioned above which is made within seven years of the persons death will be included in the value of the estate. Any gift made more than seven years from the death of the person making it is free of any liability for tax. These gifts are known as "Potentially Exempt Transfers" (PETS) and become wholly exempt once seven years have elapsed and the donor is still alive. If the donor dies within seven years of making the gift only a percentage of the tax payable will be due, depending on how long before the death it was made, in keeping with the following scale:

6-7 years   20% of gift at rate of 8%

5-6 years   40% of gift at rate of 16%

4-5 years   60% of gift at rate of 16%

3-4 years   80% of gift at rate of 32%

up to 3 years 100% of gift at rate of 40%

Life Insurance Policies

If a person has a life insurance policy on his or her life and for own benefit the value of the policy forms part of the estate. If there is a gift of the policy during that persons lifetime then the premium payment and not the policy becomes a potentially exempt transfer which will not be included in that persons estate if they survive seven years after the gift. If a policy is taken out for the benefit of another person it is the premium payment which is the PET and not the value of the policy. Policies such as this can be a useful way of making provision for inheritance tax liability on an estate as a whole.

Gifts with reservation

One way in which a person may seek to minimise inheritance tax liability is to reduce the value of the estate by making gifts before death. As demonstrated, these will be regarded as PETS and may be brought into the estate if death occurs within seven years. There is another factor to be considered. If a person gives something away but still continues to enjoy it or derive a benefit from it, then such a gift will form part of the estate whenever it was made so long as the donor continued to enjoy it up to his or her death. This is known as a "gift with reservation" because the donor reserves a benefit. To avoid a gift with reservation, the gift must be enjoyed by the person to whom it has been given.

The payment of tax

Whenever money is left in a will consideration needs to be given as to whether inheritance tax attributable to it is to be paid out of the residue of the estate or to be paid by the person receiving the legacy. If inheritance tax comes from the residue of the estate then it should be declared to be free of tax, if paid by the person to whom it is left, it is declared subject to tax.

Deductions from the estate

From the overall value of the estate for inheritance tax purposes, reasonable funeral expenses can be deducted. In addition, any additional expenses incurred in administering or realising property outside of the United Kingdom against its value (to a maximum of 50%) can be realised.

Gifts to charitable institutions

Gifts to charities are exempt at any time whether as lifetime gifts or passed under the terms of a will. They can be expressed as either to a specific charity or as an amount to be distributed by the dead persons trustees. These can be the same as the executors in which case they should be named as trustees as well as executors.

In many cases a person will make a will many years before death. This could mean that unless a will is revised regularly, the amounts of money specified as bequests may become devalued through inflation so that on death they no longer represent the original size of the gift that was intended.

One common way of overcoming this is to express the gift as a percentage or proportion of the overall net estate.

If you wish a bequest to go to a specific branch of a charity this must be specified, otherwise the gift will go to head office as a matter of course.

*****

Chapter 8

Making a Will in Scotland

There are a number of key differences for a will made in Scotland, which need to be highlighted:

- Intestacy

If you do not make a will in Scotland before you die, the law is as follows:

- If there is a spouse/civil partner but no other close family, such as children, parents, brothers and sisters etc, then the spouse benefits from the whole estate.
- If there is a spouse/civil partner and there are children, then the spouse/civil partner can have property (or £50,000 if it is worth more) furniture and personal possessions up to a value of £10,000, cash up to £15,000 and a third of the remainder of the state (excluding other property). Children (or their children) share what is left in equal proportion.
- If there is no spouse/civil partner but there are children then they or their children benefit from the estate in equal shares. (not stepchildren).

- If there is no spouse/civil partner or children, but there are parents, brothers and sisters then the parents take half of the estate and the other half is divided equally between any brothers and sisters or their children. Where only one of these groups is alive, those concerned benefit from the whole estate.

If none of the above applies, then the following benefit, in this order:

- Full uncles/aunts or their children
- Half uncles/aunts or their children
- Grandparents
- Full great uncles/aunts (or descendants)
- Half great uncles/aunts (or descendants)
- Great grandparents

If no relatives can be found then the Crown takes the estate and can distribute it among anyone with a reasonable claim.

- **Age**

Whereas in the rest of the United Kingdom you need to be over 18 to make a will, in Scotland the age limit is lower. For a male it is over fourteen and twelve for a female.

- **Marriage**

In Scotland, marriage does not revoke a will.

- **Children**

Elsewhere in the United Kingdom this applies to illegitimate and adopted children, in Scotland you have to specify their status in the will. If you have children after making a will and have not made any mention of them the will is considered null and void. A new will needs to be produced.

Presentation

If you produce the whole of your will by hand, then you do not need any witnesses. You must sign at the bottom of every page, not just the last page. If the will is not completely handwritten then you will need two witnesses.

Claims against your estate

In Scotland, the spouse/civil partner and children have more rights to claim against the estate than the rest of the United Kingdom, even if there is provision in the will to specifically exclude them. The law equally applies against any claims from others who were partly or totally dependent on the dead person before death.

****

Chapter 9

Wills in Northern Ireland

The law on wills and probate in Northern Ireland is very similar. However, the law for probate varies a little and it is these changes that are outlined below.

One major difference between England and Northern Ireland has been created by the Wills and Administration Proceedings (Northern Ireland) Order 1994 legislation.

In Northern Ireland, provided the will is actually signed after 1st January 1995, a married minor, or minors who have been married can now make a valid will. It is not possible for a married minor in England and Wales to make a valid will. The Administration of estates Act 1925 does not apply in Northern Ireland. The equivalent legislation is the Administration of Estates Act (Northern Ireland) 1955.

After someone has died and probate has been obtained, anyone can apply to see it or obtain a copy of it at the Probate Office, Royal Courts of Justice www.courtsni.gov.uk

If it is more than five years since the grant was obtained, application should be made to the Public Record Office of Northern Ireland www.proni.gov.uk.

Death of husband, wife or civil partner

In Northern Ireland, the common-law presumption of simultaneous deaths in cases where it is not certain who died first still applies. For this purpose it is often desirable to insert an express provision in a will that one spouse or civil partner is to benefit under the other's will only if he or she survives the testator by a fixed period, usually 30 days.

Executor not wishing to act

Only if the executor resides outside of Northern Ireland or resides in Northern Ireland but the Master is satisfied by Affidavit that it is desirable for a grant to be made to his attorney can a person named as an executor in a will appoint an attorney. So, when you make a will make sure that your executors are ready and willing to act.

Advertising for creditors and beneficiaries

The special procedure for formally advertising for creditors and beneficiaries in Northern Ireland requires both an advertisement in the Belfast Gazette and an Advertisement twice in each of any two daily newspapers printed in Northern Ireland. If the assets include land, the adverts should be in the Belfast Gazette and in any two newspapers circulating in the district where the land is situated. The advertisements in the papers should require any interested parties to send in particulars of their claim within a set period of time, which is not to be less than two months, and which will run from the date of publication of the last notice.

Applying for probate forms

Personal applications for probate forms should be made to the Probate and Matrimonial Office, www.courtsni.gov.uk Royal Courts of Justice in Belfast, (same website) or the District Probate Registry in Londonderry.

- If the deceased had a fixed place of abode within the counties of Fermanagh, Londonderry or Tyrone application may be made to either address.
- If the deceased resident resided elsewhere in Northern Ireland, the application must be made to the Belfast office at Lincoln Building, 27-45 Great Victoria Street, Belfast BT2 7SL.

The fees in all applications are based on the net value of the estate. Currently the fees are:
- Net estate under £10,000 Nil fee
- estate over £10,000 £200

Inheritance Tax Payments

The cheque for IHT due should be made payable to HM Revenue and Customs and the cheque for the probate office fee should be made out to Northern Ireland Court Service.

Form PA1

In Northern Ireland, it is not necessary to serve a notice on an executor who is not acting and who has not renounced. It is therefore possible for one executor to obtain probate without another even being aware that he or she is an executor.

Transfer of a property

While property is registered or unregistered as in England and Wales. Land law generally, in Northern Ireland is very different to that in England and Wales. In the case of registered land, the executors or administrators complete assent form 17. the completed form 17 is then sent to the Land Registers of Northern Ireland in Belfast at the Land and Property Services together with the land certificate, the original grant of probate or letters of administration and form 100A (Application for Registration). Both forms are available from the Land Registers and the fee is currently 75.

If the property Is subject to a mortgage, the certificate of charge with the 'vacate' or receipt sealed by the bank or building society should be lodged at the same time.

Entitlement on intestacy in Northern Ireland

The main difference between English and Northern Ireland Law about wills and probate relates to the rules on intestacy. In Northern Ireland, unlike England and Wales, no life interests are created on intestacy.

As in England, the nearest relatives in a fixed order are entitled to apply for the grant of letter of administration and if the nearest relative

71

does not wish to be an administrator, he or she can renounce the right to do so, in favour of the next nearest relative.

Deceased leaves surviving spouse or civil partner

The surviving spouse or civil partner normally becomes the administrator. Where there is a surviving spouse or civil partner, he or she is always entitled to the deceased's personal effects, no matter how great their value.

Children

If there are two or more children, the surviving spouse or civil partner only receives £250,000 and one third of the residue, with two thirds divided between the remaining children. This rule applies no matter how many children there are. If there is only one child, the surviving spouse or civil partner receives £250,000 and one half of the residue and the child receives the other half of the residue.

Where someone dies intestate without children but with one or more parents still alive, the surviving spouse or civil partner receives the first £450,000 of the estate together with half the residue. The other half of the residue passes to the parents of the intestate equally, or, if only one parent is still alive to that parent in its entirety.

Where someone dies without children and parents, but with brothers or sisters or children of the predeceased brothers and sisters, the surviving spouse or civil partner takes the first £450,000 of the estate together with half of the residue. The other half of the residue is divided between the surviving brothers and sisters. The children of a

72

predeceased brother or sister divide their parents share equally between them.

If there is no surviving spouse or civil partner, the entire estate is divided equally between the children. If any child has died before the intestate, the children of the deceased child divide their parents share between them. As in England, no distinction is made between natural or adopted children.

If there are no children but there are parents, the parents inherit the entire estate equally, or, if only one parent survives that parent inherits the entire estate.

If there are no children or parents, but brothers and sisters the entire estate is divided between the brothers and sisters, with the issue of any predeceased brother or sister taking their parents share.

****

Chapter 10

The Serviceman's Will

The minimum age limit applicable generally does not apply in the case of servicemen on active military service. These laws only apply in operational conditions-that is in a war situation.

The will itself can either be in writing or can be passed on orally to a witness. The witness can be a beneficiary and can receive gifts from the estate.

In the case of a written will this can be in handwriting and does not have to be witnessed. If the person gives verbal instructions as to how he or she wants the estate to be disposed of, all that is required is a clear intention that such instructions should be carried out if and indeed when the situation requires it.

A will can be revoked by similar means, that is by hand or mouth. This is only applicable if that person remains in the armed forces.

Where a person dies on active service, there is no inheritance tax on the estate.

****

Chapter 11

Probate - 1. Probate Generally

Probate simply means that the executor's powers to administer the estate of a dead person have been officially confirmed. A document called a "Grant of Representation" is given which enables those administering the estate to gain access to all relevant information, financial or otherwise concerning the person's estate.

Although anyone charged under a will to act on behalf of the dead persons estate has automatic authority to represent, there are certain cases where evidence of probate is required. If no will exists or no executors have been appointed, then it will be necessary to obtain "Letters of administration" which involves a similar procedure. Under common law, probate has a number of objectives. These are:

- To safeguard creditors of the deceased
- To ensure reasonable provision is made for the deceased's dependants
- To distribute the balance of the estate in accordance with the intentions of the person whose will it is.

One of the key factors affecting the need to obtain probate is how much money is involved under the terms of a will. Where the sums involved are relatively small then financial institutions and other organisations will not normally want to see evidence of probate. However, it should be remembered that no one is obliged to release anything relating to a dead persons estate unless letters of administration or documents of probate can be shown. Those responsible for administering the estate must find out from the organisations concerned what the necessary procedure is.

*****

Chapter 12

Probate 2-Applying for Probate

_____

Please refer to the standard forms at the back of this book for guidance on how to apply for probate.

If the value of the estate is under £5000 in total, it may be possible to administer the estate without obtaining probate. Generally, if the estate is worth more than £5000, you will have to apply for probate of the will or letters of administration. There are a number of reasons for this:

- Banks, building societies and National Savings are governed by the Administration of Estates (Small payments) Act 1965. This only allows them to refund individual accounts up to £5000 without production of probate.
- You cannot sell stocks, shares or land from an estate without probate, except in the case of land held in names of joint tenants where this passes on after death
- If the administration is disputed or if a person intends to make a claim as a dependant or member of the family, his or her claim is 'statute barred' six months after the grant of probate. The right to take action remains open if the estate is administered without probate

- A lay executor who managed to call in the assets of an estate without probate might miss the obligation to report matters to HMRC for inheritance tax purposes, especially where a substantial gift had been made in the seven years prior to the death.

Letters of administration

If someone dies intestate (without making a will) the rules of intestacy laid down by Act of Parliament will apply. These were outlined earlier. An administrator must apply for letters of administration for exactly the same reasons as the executor applies for probate. The grant of letters of administration will be made to the first applicant.

If a will deals with part only but not all of the administration (for example where the will defines who receives what but does not name an executor) the person entitled to apply for letters of administration make the application to the Registrar attaching the will at the same time. The applicant is granted 'Letters of administration with will attached'.

Applying for letters of administration

The following demonstrates the order of those entitled to apply:

- The surviving spouse/civil partner (not unmarried partner)
- The children or their descendants (once over 18)
- If there are no children or descendants of those children who are able to apply, the parents of the deceased can apply
- Brothers and sisters 'of the half blood'
- Grandparents

- Aunts and uncles of the whole blood
- Aunts and uncles of the half blood
- The Crown (or Duchy of Lancaster or Duchy of Cornwall) if there are no blood relation

Where the estate is insolvent other creditors have the right to apply.

The probate registry – applying for probate

The first step is to obtain the necessary forms from the personal application department of the Principal Probate Registry in London or the local district probate registry. The more straightforward cases can usually be handled by post or by one visit to the probate registry. The executor will complete and send in the forms, they are checked and the amount of probate fees and inheritance tax assessed. The registry officials prepare the official document which the executor then swears, attending personally to do so. The process from submission to swearing usually takes three to four weeks.

Filling in the forms

The necessary forms for applying for probate can be obtained from the probate registry. These are:

- Form PA1 – the probate application form
- Form 1HT 205 – the return of assets and debts

With the forms you will receive other items which serve as guidance to the forms and process:

- 1HT 206 – notes to help you with 1HT 205

- Form PA1 (A) – guidance notes for completing PA1
- Form PA3 – a list of local probate offices
- Form PA4 – a table of fees payable

Form PA1 is fairly uncomplicated. The form is split into white and blue sections with the applicant filling in the white sections. The form will ask which office the applicant wants to attend, details of the deceased, the will and something about you. In cases where more than one executor is involved, the registrar will usually correspond with one executor only. The form also has a space for naming any executors who cannot apply for probate, e.g. because they do not want to or have died since the will was written. If they may apply at a later date, the probate office will send an official 'power reserved letter' which the non-acting executor signs. This is a useful safeguard in case the first executor dies or becomes incapacitated before grant of probate is obtained.

You do not have to sign form PA1. At the end of the process, the probate registry will couch the information you supply in legal jargon for the document you are required to sign.

Form PA1 contains a reminder that you have to attach the death certificate, the will and the completed form 1HT 205. If this form demonstrates that the estate exceeds the 'excepted estate' threshold (for inheritance tax purposes) form 1HT 200 will have to be completed.

Sending the forms

If the estate you are administering can be contained on form 1HT 205, you are ready to send in your application. Make sure that you take photocopies of all material. You should send the following:

- The will
- The death certificate
- Probate application form PA1
- Short form 1HT 205
- A cheque for the fee

Attach any explanatory letter as necessary. You should then send the package by registered post. A few weeks later, you will be invited to review the documents, pay the probate fee and swear the prescribed oath. Remember to take your file of background papers.

Probate fees are calculated on the amount of the net estate, as declared for the purpose of inheritance tax. Fees are payable when you attend the interview at the registry – see form PA4 for guidance.

Attendance at the probate registry
When you arrive at the probate registry you will need to examine the forms that have been prepared for you. You need to satisfy yourself that all the details are correct. When you have checked all the details, the commissioner will ask you to sign the original will and swear the oath, identifying the will as that of the deceased.

The actual process entails you standing up, holding a copy of the New Testament and repeating the words spoken by the commissioner. The words take the form of 'I swear by Almighty God that this is my name and handwriting and that the contents of this my oath are true and that this is the will referred to'. The form of oath is varied depending on religious belief or otherwise.

The commissioner will then sign beneath your signature on the official form and will. The fees are paid and any sealed copies as ordered will be supplied.

Inheritance tax and form 1HT 200

Form 1HT 200 is the HMRC account for inheritance tax. It should be completed by reference to form 1HT 210, guidance notes. 1HT consists of eight pages. Take time and care with this form. It is relatively uncomplicated. Please refer to the appendix for an example.

The grant of probate

There may be a time lapse of six weeks or more between lodging the probate papers and the meeting at the registry to sign and swear them. After this has happened, however, things move quickly. If there is no inheritance tax to be paid – where the net estate is less than £325,000, or where the deceased property goes to the spouse – the grant of probate (or letters of administration) is issued within a few days. If Inheritance tax Is due, It takes two to three weeks before the exact amount is calculated and the grant is usually ready about a week later. The grant of probate is signed by an officer of the probate registry. Attached to the grant of probate is a photocopy of the will. (All original wills are kept at the Principal Probate Registry in London). Each page of your copy of the will carries the impress of the courts official seal. It is accompanied by a note which explains the procedure for collecting and distributing the estate and advises representatives to take legal advice in the event of dispute or other difficulty.

Chapter 13

Administering Estates

___

There are a number of sample letters contained as appendix three to this book which will be of use when administering the estate of the deceased.

The formalities

Relatives or friends of the deceased will take on the task of dealing with the necessary formalities after death. In the first instance, notwithstanding where the person dies, a doctor must provide relatives with a certificate stating the cause of death. This certificate is then lodged at the Registry of Births Deaths and marriages within five days of the issue. The registrar will need to know full details of the death and will also ask for any other certificates such as marriage and birth. The person who registers the death is known as the 'informant'.

If the doctor states that the cause of death is uncertain, then the arrangements are rather more complex. The death will first be reported to the coroner, who usually orders a post-mortem. If it shows that the cause of death was natural, the coroner then authorises the burial or cremation. In these cases, you will be issued with a death certificate by the Registrar and a second certificate permitting the undertaker to arrange burial or cremation.

Except in rare cases, for example violent death when the coroner orders an inquest to be held, it will now be time to organise the funeral. It will be necessary at this point to check the will or if there is no will, to find out about the arrangements for administering the estate.

Funeral arrangements

If there is a will in existence, it may well contain details concerning the desired funeral arrangements of the deceased. If there are no clear instructions the executors of the will usually make appropriate arrangements. The executor will become legally liable to pay costs of the funeral.

Where the deceased dies intestate, the 'administrators' of the estate will instruct the undertaker and assume responsibility for payments. In some cases, it may be clear that the deceased does not have enough assets to cover the funeral. If this is the case then investigations need to take place, including the possibility of a one-off funeral grant to cover costs. Once financial details have been settled it is advisable to put a notice in the deaths column of one or more papers to bring the funeral to the attention of relatives.

The responsibilities of executors

Executors and administrators of estates have very important responsibilities. In the first instance they are responsible for ensuring that the assets of the estate are paid to the correct beneficiaries of the will and also for ensuring that all debts are paid before distribution. If this aspect of administration is mismanaged then the executor or

85

administrator will be held, or could be held, liable for any debts. In order to ensure that they are protected then executors or administrators should advertise in the London gazette – which is a newspaper for formal notices of any kind, and also a local paper together with requests that creditors should submit their claims by a date which must be at least two months after the advertisement. Private individuals will usually have to produce a copy of probate before their advertisement is accepted for publication. (See sample letters appendix three)The executor's initial steps

If you are the executor of a valid will (or if you are the administrator if there is no will) you can now begin the task of administering the estate. It will be essential to ensure that the basic elements are dealt with such as informing utilities, arranging for termination of certain insurance policies and discharge of liabilities of others such as life insurance. Arrangements will need to be made for any pets and post redirected. These are the basic essential lifestyle elements before you make an application for probate.

The value of the estate

Before you can apply for probate of the will, you have to find out the extent and value of the assets and liabilities of the estate. You will need to have access to all records of assets, such as insurance policies and bank accounts. The ease with which you can establish a total value will depend on how organised the deceased was. If the deceased was a taxpayer it is advisable to approach the local tax office for a copy of his or her last tax return, sending a copy of the will to prove your status as an executor.

Once you have collated all proof of assets including property you will need to arrive at a total value. The following will provide a pointer for establishing value:

Bank accounts

Interest-bearing accounts and joint bank accounts

When you have found out details of these accounts you should ask for details of balance and accrued interest at the time of death. This is needed for the tax return you will have to complete on behalf of the deceased estate. (See sample letters)

These types of accounts can be problematic. If the joint holders are husband and wife/civil partners, the account will pass automatically to the survivor. In other cases you will need to establish the intentions of the joint owners or the contribution of each to the joint account. This is because the amount contributed by the deceased forms part of the estate for tax purposes (except where a written agreement confirms that the money in the account passes automatically to the survivor). In the case of business partnership accounts, you need a set of final trading accounts to the date of death and should contact the surviving partner.

National Savings

These may take the form of National Savings Certificates, National Savings Investment Accounts or Premium Bonds. A claim form for repayment should be obtained, usually from the post office and sent to the appropriate department for National Savings together with a copy of the probate when you have it.

Building societies

You would approach a building society in the same way as a bank, asking for a balance and interest to date. You should also ask for a claim form for payment.

Life insurance

You should write to insurance companies stating the date of death and the policy number and enclose a copy of the death certificate. Once probate has been obtained submit your claim form for monies owed. In many cases, policies are held on trust and will not form part of an estate. Insurance companies will, on production of the death certificate, make payment direct to the beneficiaries.

Stock and shares

You should make arrangements to forward a list of stocks and shares held by the deceased to a bank or stockbroker. In the case of Pep's and ISA's you should send them to the plan manger and ask for a valuation. Ask for transfer forms for all shareholdings. You may decide to value the stocks and shares yourself. If this is the case, you will need a copy of the official Stock Exchange Daily Official List for the day on which the deceased died. The valuation figure is calculated by adding 25% of the difference between the selling and buying prices. If the death took place at the weekend you can choose either the Monday or Friday Valuation.

However, if the executors sell any shares at a loss within 12 months, the selling price in all cases can be taken as the value at the date of death.

If you cannot locate all of the share certificates, you may be able to find dividend counterfoils or tax vouchers among the papers of the deceased which will enable you to check the number of shares held in the company. If you cannot find share certificates, write to the Registrar of the company. Name of Registrars are given in the Register of Registrars held in the local library. The same approach can be made if the deceased holds unit trusts. In the case of private companies where no value of shares is published, you may sometimes be able to obtain a valuation from the secretary of the company. In the case of a family company it will usually be necessary to have the value determined by a private accountant. (see sample letters)

Pensions

If the deceased was already receiving a pension, you should write to the company operating the scheme in order to find out further details, i.e. Is the pension paid up until the time of death, are there any other beneficiaries after death and so on? Pensions vary significantly and it is very important that accurate information is obtained.

State benefits

If the deceased was in receipt of an old age pension, notice of the death should be given to the Department of Work and Pensions, so that any adjustments can be made. In the case of married men, the agency will make arrangements to begin to pay widows pension.

Businesses

The valuation of a business on the death of one of the partners is complicated and depends upon the nature of the business, the way in which the accounts are prepared and the extent of the assets held by the business. The surviving partner/s should make available a set of partnership accounts to the date of death and help you to determine the correct valuation for the deceased share.

Farms

If the deceased had an interest in a farm, any type of farm you should seek advice of a more specialist agricultural valuer.

Residential property

If the estate is below the inheritance tax threshold, you may be able to estimate the value of the property by looking at similar properties in estate agents windows. You may also wish to obtain a professional valuation. If the estate reaches the inheritance tax threshold or is close to it, the figure is checked by the District Valuer. If the property is sold within four years of death for less than the probate valuation, and providing the sellers are executors and not beneficiaries, the sale price may be substituted for the original valuation.

In the case of joint properties, the value of the person who has died forms part of the estate for tax purposes. However, if the share passes to the spouse/civil partner, the 'surviving spouse exemption' applies. This means that there is no inheritance tax to pay, even if the estate exceeds the inheritance tax threshold.

If there is a mortgage on the property at the date of death, the amount of the debt must be found by writing to the bank or building society. The value of the house is reduced by this amount.

Where the deceased has left residential property as a specific item, the will may either say that the property is to be transferred to the beneficiary free from any mortgage or that it is subject to a mortgage, The Administration of Estates Act provides that a person who is bequeathed a mortgaged property is responsible repaying the mortgage unless the will sets out a contrary intention.

With other property and buildings-If the deceased owned commercial property, the executor has to determine whether this was a business asset or whether it is an investment property unconnected with any business. If this is the case a separate valuation will be needed.

Personal possessions

Although it is not always necessary to obtain professional valuations for household goods, estimated values are examined very carefully by the District Valuer, if the estate is large enough to attract Inheritance tax. The way household goods are dealt with will depend entirely on their value. In certain cases, with items such as painting and jewelry then an auction may be appropriate.

Income tax

It is very unlikely that, before you make your application for probate, you will be in a position to calculate the income tax owed on an estate. As the administration of the estate gathers momentum then you will amass enough information to start forming a picture of the value and thus the tax liabilities. (see sample letters to HMRC)

*****

Chapter 14

The Distribution of an Estate

The distribution of the estate of the deceased

Having established probate, it is now time to begin to distribute the estate. Before you can do this, however, it is essential that you understand exactly what the will says. The executor can be sued for payment if the estate is not distributed exactly in accordance with the stipulations in the will. Although this may sound like common sense, some wills may be couched in a particular way, or in a particular jargon and you may need advice on the interpretation.

Specific legacies and bequests

Legacies are, usually, the payment of specific sums of money. Bequests usually mean gifts of goods or cash. 'Devises' means gifts of land or buildings. If the state is not subject to inheritance tax and the legacies and bequests are small, legacies can be paid without further delay and also specific items can be handed over. It is advisable to obtain a receipt from the beneficiary(s) when they receive their gift or legacy. One common problem that can arise is trying to trace beneficiaries. This is usually done through the local or national press if the beneficiary is not forthcoming.

Transferring property

If a beneficiary has been left a house or other property then any outstanding debts relating to the property, such as a mortgage have to be dealt with. The will usually directs the executors to pay off the mortgage. However, if the will is silent on this point then it will become the responsibility of the beneficiary. It is quite usual that a property is left to another with a mortgage and equity in the property so the beneficiary can continue to pay.

It will be necessary to transfer the property into your own name by contacting the Land Registry. If the property is already registered, as is most property, the process will be straightforward. However, if it is unregistered then you will need to obtain a first registration. You would probably need to instruct a solicitor to do this. At the same time obtain advice about settling the mortgage.

Preparation of final accounts

Having gathered the assets and obtained a good idea of the value you can now begin to prepare final accounts. There is no set form for the final accounts but assets and liabilities must be included, receipts and payments made during the administration and a distribution account of payments to beneficiaries.

It is helpful to include a covering sheet to the accounts, a form of memorandum which will cover the following areas:

- Details of the deceased and date of death, date of probate and names of executors
- A summary of the bequests made in the will

94

- Particulars of property transfers
- Reference to any valuations which have been included in the accounts

In estates where inheritance tax has been paid, you should prepare one part of the capital account based on the value of the assets at the time of death.

The second part of the account should demonstrate the value of those assets and liabilities at the date they are realised or paid. If the net effect is to reduce the value of the estate, you may be able to claim a refund from the capital taxes office. Conversely you may have increased taxes to pay. In either case you should advise the capital taxes office.

A model set of accounts are shown in the appendix. The capital account shows the value of assets when they are cashed or realised and the debts are the sums actually paid. The income account shows the income received during the administration, less associated expenses. It is convenient to run this account from the date of death to the following 5th of April.

The distribution account shows the capital and income transferred from the respective accounts and how the residue of the estate has been divided. If there is only one beneficiary you should show the final figure. If any items have been taken in kind – such as a car or a piece of furniture – its value is included in the distribution account as both an asset and payment. If you are claiming executor's expenses itemise them and include them in the distribution account.

Where a will exists

When you have completed your accounts, and all outstanding debts and liabilities have been met, you will now be in a position to calculate how much each residuary beneficiary receives according to the specific provisions of the will. In practice, the amount that you have left in the executor's bank account should match the sums to be paid out.

After having ascertained that this is the case, and rectified any errors you should send the accounts to the beneficiaries for their agreement or otherwise. In cases involving inheritance tax, you should contact the capital taxes office and confirm that you have disclosed the full value of the estate. You then apply for a clearance certificate. When you have received this you can make the final distribution to the beneficiaries. The beneficiaries should be asked to sign an acknowledgement that they agree the accounts and that they agree the amount that they will receive.

Where beneficiaries are deceased or missing

If a beneficiary dies before the death of the testator, the general rule is that the legacy cannot be made. There are a few exceptions to this rule:

- If the will contains a 'substitution' (an alternative to the beneficiary)
- If the gift is made to two people as joint tenants – the survivor being the beneficiary
- If section 33(2) of the Wills Act 1837 applies. This section provides that, if the share of the estate or gift is to a child or other descendant of the testator and the child dies before the testator leaving 'issue' (children and their descendants) they take the share of the gift.

96

If a beneficiary cannot be located, you must take steps to find that person. These steps must be reasonable. As stated, an advertisement can suffice, as well as contacting relatives and so on. You can apply to the court for an order giving you permission to distribute the estate on agreed terms. You can also claim any expenses incurred from the estate.

It is very important, if you cannot find a beneficiary that you take steps to obtain a court order in order to protect yourself from any future problems arising should a beneficiary turn up.

Beware!

As discussed in the introduction to this book, in addition to will writing companies, firms of unregulated "Heir Hunters" have grown up which chase missing beneficiaries and charge extortionate fees before handing over a legacy. Although there are decent companies who earn their reasonable fees, there are companies which can cause more trouble than they are worth. The advice is for any beneficiary is to avoid such companies if they won't reveal the name of the relative before making demand for payment. Beneficiaries should research recent deaths at bonavacantia.gov.uk, (which is a list published by the government of people who have died without a will or next of kin). Look for the names of known relatives or of people with family surnames. If you know your relationship to any such person use the form on the website to enter a claim. If you suspect but don't know of a relationship use a professional genealogist at an hourly rate, usually for a few hours work.

**

The children's trust under intestacy rules We saw earlier in the book how an estate is distributed according to the rules of intestacy. When the surviving spouse has children, whatever their age, and the estate is worth more than £125,000, the administrators of the estate must set up a trust to look after the children's share. As trustees, they must invest half the remaining capital in their own names. They notify HMRC of the new trust and submit a Trust Tax return each year. The income from the trust is paid to the spouse. On the death of the spouse, the capital held in the trust account is shared between the children unless they are under 18.

If any of the children die, leaving children of their own, before the death of the intestate or — whichever is the later — second parent, the Statutory Trust rules apply. Under these rules, where a child of the intestate has died leaving children who are 18 or over (or who marry before 18) the children get their parents share. The same applies if the only survivors are grandchildren or even remote descendants.

*****

Glossary of terms

Administrator

The person who administers the estate of a person who has died intestate

Bequest

A gift of a particular object or cash as opposed to 'devise' which means land or buildings

Chattels

Personal belongings of the deceased

Child

Referred to in a will or intestacy – child of the deceased including adopted and illegitimate children but, unless specifically included in a will, not stepchildren

Cohabitee

A partner of the deceased who may be able to claim a share of the estate. The term 'common law wife' has no legal force.

Confirmation

The document issued to executors by the sheriff court in Scotland to authorise them to administer the estate

Devise

A gift of house or land

Disposition

A formal conveyancing document in Scotland

Estate

All the assets and property of the deceased, including houses, cars, investments, money and personal belongings

Executor

The person appointed in the will to administer the estate of a deceased person

Heritable estate

Land and buildings in Scotland

Inheritance tax

The tax which may be payable when the total estate of the deceased person exceeds a set threshold (subject to various exemptions and adjustments)

Intestate

A person who dies without making a will

Issue

Al the descendants of a person, i.e. children, grandchildren, great grandchildren#

Legacy

A gift of money

Minor

A person under 18 years of age

Moveable estate

Property other than land or buildings in Scotland

Next of Kin

The person entitled to the estate when a person dies intestate

Letters of administration

The document issued to administrators by a probate registry to authorise them to administer the estate of an intestate

Personal estate or personalty

Al the investments and belongings of a person apart from land and buildings

Personal representatives

A general term for both administrators and executors

Probate of the will

The document issued to executors by a probate registry in England, Wales and Northern Ireland to authorise them to administer the estate

Probate Registry

The Government office which deals with probate maters. The principal Probate Registry is in London with district registries in cities and some large towns

Real estate or realty

Land and buildings owned by a person

Residue

What is left of the estate to share out after all the debts and specific bequests and legacies have been paid

Specific bequests

Particular items gifted by will

Testator

A person who makes a will

Will

The document in which you say what is to happen to your estate after death

****

Useful Addresses

Department for National Savings

Glasgow G58 1SB

www.nsandi.com

08085 007 007

Pensions Advisory Service

11 Belgrave Road

London

SW1V 1RB

www.pensionsadvisoryservice.org.uk

0300 1043 1047

The Law Society of England and Wales

113 Chancery lane

London WC2A 1PL

0207 242 1222

Public information including solicitors who specialise in wills and probate

www.lawsociety.org.uk

London Gazette

PO Box 7923

London SE1 5ZH

0333 200 2434

www.thegazette.co.uk

www.solicitors-online.com

Information on solicitors specialising in wills and probate

The London Probate Department

First Avenue House

42-49 High Holborn

London WC1V 6NP

Email enquiries

londonprobate@hmcts.gsi.gov.uk

Probate helpline:

0300 123 1072

Enquiries:

0207 421 8509

Useful Addresses in Scotland

Accountant of Court

Hadrian House

Callendar Business park

Callendar Road

Falkirk

FK1 1XR Tel 01324 678303

www.scotscourts.gov.uk

Law Society of Scotland

Atria One, 144 Morrison St,

Edinburgh,

EH3 8EX

0131 476 7411

www.lawsoct.org.uk

Northern Ireland

Age NI Ireland Northern Ireland

7 West Street, Carrickfergus BT38 7AR

 028 9336 01

District Public Registry

The Court House

Bishop Street

Londonderry

BT48 7PY

0208 7126 1832

HM Revenue and Customs Capital taxes

(Northern Ireland)

www.nidirect.gov.uk

Law Society of Northern Ireland

40 Linenhall Street

Belfast

BT2 8BA

028 902 31614

www.lawsoc.ni.org

Probate Office

Royal Courts of Justice

Chichester Street

Belfast

BT1 3JF

028 9072 4678

www.courtsni.gov.uk

Public Record Office of Northern Ireland

https://www.nidirect.gov.uk/proni

****

Appendix 1 Example of Administration Accounts

In the Estate of   Deceased.

Date of death

CAPITAL ACCOUNT

Assets

House Net sales proceeds	£145,000
(value at death £155,000)	
Less mortgage	£95,000
	£50,000
Stocks and shares	£89,000
(value at death £86500)	
Life policy	£7500
Skipton BS deposit	£9000
Interest to date of death	£75
National Savings – Premium bonds	£7000
Arrears of pension	£325
Agreed value of house contents	£3800
Car	£5600
Gross estate	£172,300

Less debts and liabilities

Funeral costs	£2000
Gas	£270
Electricity	£25
Administration expenses	£45
Probate fees	£130
Stockbrokers valuation fee	£250
Income tax paid to date of death	£650

Inheritance tax paid on application for probate (N/a) estate less than £240,000

Net Estate carried to distribution account

£168930

For the estate to attract inheritance tax the value would need to be above £325,000. If that is the case, carry on the calculation for inheritance tax by multiplying the residue after £325,000 by 40% which will give you the inheritance tax due.

In the estate of   Deceased

Income account

Dividends received for period from 1st October 20t o 5th April 20

Holding	Company	Net dividend
5000 shares	ABC PLC	£1400

4300 shares	Halifax PLC	£560
12000 shares	GKN	£1420
3760 shares	Powergen	£420
Savings accounts final interest		£150
Balance transferred to distribution account		
		£3950

In the estate of   Deceased

Distribution account

Balance transferred from capital account	£168930
Balance transferred from income account	£3950
	£172880

Less payment of legacies

David Peters	£5000
Net residuary estate for distribution	£167880

Mr Frederick Dillon

A one half share represented by

a)	House contents	£3800
b)	The balance	£80140

109

Stella Donaldson

One half share represented by the balance   £83940

Total   _____

                                                                £167880

                                                    ****

Appendix 2

sample letters wills and probate-cross section of letters to send when administering estates of deceased persons

Sample letter which should accompany the advertisement for creditors and claimants-local newspaper

---

The   Daily Times

Dear Sirs/Madam

In respect of   Deceased

Further to our discussions, please find enclosed an advertisement pursuant to Section 27 of the Trustee Act 1925. Please insert this into your newspaper for one week only.

Yours faithfully

Letter to the London Gazette requesting form for advertising for claimants and creditors.

To: The Manager
the London Gazette
PO Box 7923
London SE1 5ZH

Dear Sir/Madam

Could you please send me a form for completion to enable me to have an advertisement placed in the London Gazette pursuant to section 27 of the Trustees Act 1925. Please let me have a note of any fees payable to you.

Yours faithfully

To The London Gazette enclosing a form for advertisement for claimants and creditors

To: The Manager
the London Gazette
PO Box 7923
London SE1 5ZH

Dear Sir/Madam
Re: The Deceased

Please find enclosed an advertisement for claimants and creditors plus office copy of grant of representation for inspection and return, along with a cheque for payment. Please publish the advertisement in the first available issue of the Gazette.

Yours faithfully

Letters to be sent pre-grant of probate

Letters to banks and building societies

The manager
(Bank/Building Society)

Dear Sir/Madam

I am the executor/administrator of the estate of your customer (insert name and address plus account numbers as appropriate). This person passed away on the   and I enclose a registrar's death certificate and a copy of the will (if there is a will).

Please could you let me have any details of accounts, all accounts, which the deceased has with your organisation, particulars of any assets or securities held for safe custody plus any other financial documents which will be relevant in forming a picture of the estate.

Please forward the following in respect of each account held in the deceased's name:

1. balance of account as at the date of death plus any interest owed.

2. Interest accrued to the account between the end of the last financial year and the date of death.

3. Whether the interest is paid gross or net.

4. Whether there are any direct debits or standing orders in respect of each account. please supply particulars.

Any other credit balances on non-interest bearing accounts in the deceased's sole name should be placed on deposit until production of the grant of probate has been given.

Can you let me know your requirements for closing the accounts in the deceased's sole name, and let me have any necessary forms. Please confirm that any accounts held jointly can continue to be operated by the surviving account holder.

Please cancel any standing orders in respect of the accounts and do not meet any further direct debits.

Please send all future communications to me at the above address, please do not hesitate to contact me on the above phone number.

Please find enclosed (passbooks etc).

Yours faithfully

Letter to registrars of companies in respect of stocks and shares

To: The Registrar (Company name address)

Dear Sir/madam

Re: (Deceased) (Company name and share account number etc)

I am the personal representative of   and I enclose a death certificate for your attention. Please register and return.

Can you please confirm the extent of the deceased's holding and let me have the transfer deeds for completion to enable the transfer to beneficiaries when probate is obtained.

Yours faithfully

Letter to Stockbrokers

To: (Company name address)

Dear Sir/madam

I am the personal representative of   and I enclose a death certificate for your attention. Please register and return.

Please let me have a statement of the deceased nominee account with you as at the date of death specifying the deceased holdings and cash position. This is for the purposes of distribution on obtaining probate.

Yours faithfully

Letter to creditors

To: (Insert name and address of creditor)

Dear Sir/Madam

Re: Account number

I am the executor/proposed administrator of the estate of who died on and I enclose a death certificate for your records. Please return original.

Please let me have a final statement detailing the amount claimed. Please note, in light of the fact that the debtor has died, please take no enforcement action until the estate is in funds, probate is granted and distributions made.

All future correspondence re the deceased should be sent to the above address.

Yours faithfully

Letter to employer

To (employer)

Attention of the payroll department

Deaf Sir/Madam

Re: (Deceased) (Payroll number if known)

I am the executor/administrator of the above estate who died on
and who was employed by your company as
I enclose a death certificate for your records please return the original.

Please supply the following:

1. Whether any salary is due to the above and your requirements for them to be claimed.

2. The gross amount of salary paid in the current financial year and income tax paid.

3. Whether the above was a member of a pension fund. if so, please supply details.

4. The name and address of the tax district relevant to the deceased.

All future communications should be sent to me at the above address.

Yours faithfully

Letter to HMRC in respect of Income tax

To HM Inspector of Taxes

(Name and Address)

Insert tax reference if known

Dear Sir/Madam

I am the executor/administrator of the estate of (Deceased) who died on   I enclose a death certificate for your records. please copy and return the original.

Please supply me with a copy of the deceased's last tax return and the appropriate forms to enable me to make a return to the date of death and in due course a personal representative's return for the period to the finalisation of the estate.

Please let me have details of any tax outstanding or any repayments due to the deceased and your requirements to enable these matters to be dealt with.

Please address all future communications to me at the above address.

Yours faithfully

Letter to mortgage company

To: The Manager (name and address of company)

Dear Sir/madam
(Mortgage reference address of property mortgaged and name of deceased)

I am the executor/administrator of the above named customer who died on   I enclose a death certificate for you to copy and return the original.

Can you please let me know the capital amount outstanding on the account to the date of death. Please also let me know the amount of interest outstanding at the date of death.

Please let me have details of any endowment policy and the company involved. The grant of representation will be registered with you when it has been granted and I will then let you know the position concerning the mortgage, i.e. whether it is to be paid off or continued in the beneficiaries name.

Until that time, please see that no enforcement action be taken. Please send all correspondence to the above address.

Yours faithfully

Letter to pension fund where pension is already being paid

To: The Secretary

(Name and address)

Dear Sir/madam

Insert details of pension number name etc

I am the executor/administrator of the estate of   who

died on   I enclose a death certificate which should be

copied with the original returned.

Please let me know:

1. Whether there are any arrears of pension due to the estate to

the date of death or any overpaid pension due to be refunded to

the pension fund.

2. Your requirements to enable you to pay any arrears.

3. the gross amount of pension payable in the current tax year,

including sums to the date of death but not yet paid.

4. the amount of tax deducted or which will be deducted from the

current tax years pension.

5. the address and reference number for the relevant tax district.

All communications re the above should now be addressed to me.

Yours faithfully

To pension fund where pension is not yet being paid

The Secretary

(name and address)

Dear Sir/madam

Re: (Deceased) (pension number)

I am the executor/administrator of the estate of   who is a contributor to a pension fund administered by you. The deceased passed away on   and I enclose a death certificate for your records. please return the original.

I understand that the deceased, who was employed by   was a member of your scheme. Please let me know what benefits are due to the deceased's estate and dependants and whether the benefits are subject to inheritance tax. Please send all correspondence concerning the deceased to the above address.

Yours faithfully

Post Grant of Representation

Banks and building societies

To: The Manager
Address

Dear Sir/madam

Name and account number

Further to my recent correspondence to you, please find an office copy grant of probate/letters of administration for your records. please note and return.

I enclose the completed withdrawal forms for your attention.

Please close the account and let me have a remittance for the sum due together with a final statement of account.

Yours faithfully

To registrars in respect of shares and stock (certificated holdings)

To: the registrar

Name and address

Dear Sir/madam

Re: Deceased name and address reference number

I am the personal representative of   and I enclose an office copy of grant of representation for your records and to return. I also enclose the relevant certificates together with the un-cashed (dividend/interest) warrant(s) in respect of the holdings set out below.

Please amend or reissue the warrants in my name so that they can be paid into the estates bank account. Please endorse the certificates so that they can be sold.

Yours faithfully

Stock brokers

To

name and address

Dear Sirs

Re: (name and reference number if known)

I am the personal representative of   and I enclose an office copy of grant of representation for registration and return in respect of the deceased's holdings in (name of relevant companies)

Please transfer/sell the holdings as follows (set out details of the required transfers or sales for each company stating the relevant number of shares or amount of stock, and name and address of each transferee if transfers are required).

Yours faithfully

Creditors paying account

To

Name and address

Dear Sirs

Re: My previous communication in respect of

I enclose a cheque in the sum of   in settlement of your enclosed account. Please send a receipt as soon as possible.

Yours faithfully

Inspector of taxes notifying end of administration period and enclosing final tax return

---

To: HM Inspector of Taxes

Name and address

tax reference

Dear Sir/madam

Re: (Deceased details)

No further income is anticipated in respect of the above estate. Accordingly, please find enclosed the final tax return in respect of the estate, together with the certificates of deduction of tax from your income. Please return the certificates to me in due course.

Please let me have a final tax assessment in respect of the estate.

I shall be obliged if you will also let me have (number required) forms R185E in respect of the beneficiaries.

Yours faithfully

Letter to capital tax office requesting inheritance tax clearance.

To: Capital taxes

Farrers House

PO Box 38

Castle Meadow Road

Nottingham

NG2 1BB

Dear Sir/Madam

Re: (Capital taxes reference, deceased details)

I would be grateful if you would let me have a formal inheritance tax clearance at your earliest convenience.

Yours faithfully

Letter to residuary beneficiaries enclosing accounts for approval

To: (name and address of beneficiary)

Dear

Re: the estate of (deceased)

The administration of the estate of the above has now been completed and I enclose copies of accounts in duplicate for your approval. Accounts have also been sent to the other parties fro their approval.

If you approve the accounts, please sign and date the form of discharge at the bottom of one copy and return that copy to me.

When all parties have returned the accounts to me approved I will be in a position to let you have a remittance for monies due to you.

If you have any queries please do not hesitate to contact me.

Yours faithfully

Appendix 3 – Example forms to be used in the process of probate

1. PA2-HOW TO OBTAIN PROBATE-GUIDE FOR THE APPLICANT WITHOUT SOLICITOR.
2. APPLICATION FOR A PROBATE SEARCH

How to obtain probate -

A guide for people acting without a solicitor

What is the Probate Service?

The Probate Service is part of HM Courts & Tribunals Service. It administers the system of probate in England and Wales, and issues grants of representation, which give people the legal right to handle the estate (for example, money, possessions and property) of a deceased person.

This leaflet provides guidance if you want to obtain probate without using a solicitor.

If you have any queries, please contact your local probate registry (see leaflet **PA4**). The staff are there to help you – but they cannot give you legal advice.

Introduction

When a person dies, they usually leave an estate (including money, possessions and property).

In order to access the estate, the personal representative(s) of the deceased need to apply to the Probate Service for a grant of representation (a grant). The grant establishes who can legally collect money from banks, building societies and other organisations which hold assets belonging to the deceased person.

In most cases, applying for a grant is a straightforward procedure. It will involve completing a form with supporting documents, and swearing an oath in support of the application.

The information in this leaflet refers only to the law in England and Wales. If the deceased person was permanently resident in any other country when they died, please contact your nearest probate registry for guidance.

What is the purpose of the grant of representation?

A grant establishes who can legally collect money from banks, building societies and other organisations which hold assets belonging to the deceased person. There are three types of grant:

Probate

Probate is issued by the Probate Service to the executor(s) named in a will left by the deceased.

Letters of Administration (with will)

Letters of Administration (with will) are issued when no executor is named in the will, or when the executors are unable or unwilling to apply for the grant.

Letters of Administration

Letters of Administration are issued when the deceased person has not made a will, or the will they have made is not valid.

Is a grant always needed?

Not every estate needs a grant. A grant may not be needed if:

- the home is held in joint names and is passing by survivorship to the other joint owner(s).
- there is a joint bank or building society account. In this case, the bank may only need to see the death certificate, in order to arrange for the money to be transferred solely to the other joint owner. However, a grant could still be needed to access assets held in accounts not held in joint names, or insurance policies.
- the amount held in each account was small (even if held in the deceased's sole name). You will need to check with the organisations (banks, building societies or insurance companies) involved to find out if they will release the assets without a grant.

You may wish to ask anyone holding the deceased's money (such as a bank or insurance company) whether they will release it to you without seeing a grant. If they agree, they may attach conditions such as asking you to sign a statutory declaration before a solicitor. You will then be able to decide whether it is cheaper or easier to do this than to apply for a grant.

Please note that a grant **must** be presented in order to sell or transfer a property held in the deceased's sole name or a share of a property held jointly with the deceased and one or more other people as tenants-in-common. Tenancy-in-common is a written agreement between two or more people who own a joint asset (usually land or buildings). If you aren't sure about this you may wish to consult a solicitor.

You cannot complete a sale on any property owned, or partly owned, by a deceased person until the grant has been issued. It is therefore advisable not to put properties owned, or partly owned by the deceased, up for sale until a grant has been issued.

Who can apply for probate?

You can apply for a grant if you are over the age of 18 and:

- you are an executor named in the will;
- you are named in the will to receive some or all of the estate (if there are no executors, or if the executors are unable or unwilling to apply); or

- the deceased person did not make a will and you are their next of kin, in the following order of priority:

- lawful husband or wife or civil partner (a civil partnership is defined as a partnership between two people of the same sex which has been registered in accordance with the Civil Partnership Act 2004). The surviving partner of co-habiting couples not in a marriage or civil partnership are not entitled to apply for a grant.

- sons or daughters (excluding step-children) including children adopted by the deceased. (Children adopted out of their biological family can only apply in the estates of their adoptive parents and not their biological parents.)

- parents

- brothers or sisters

- grandparents

- uncles or aunts

- If sons, daughters, brothers, sisters, uncles or aunts of the deceased person have died before the deceased, their children may apply for a grant.

Usually, only one of the personal representatives is required to apply for a grant. However, if the person entitled to the estate is under 18, two people are legally required to apply for a grant. If this is the case we will let you know when we receive your application.

When more than one person wants to apply for a grant, they may make a joint application. A maximum of four applicants is allowed and they will all have to swear an oath in support of their application.

When you submit your application we will check to ensure that the right person(s) are applying for the grant. If you are a distant relative, please supply a brief family tree showing your relationship to the deceased person.

Where might the will be stored?

The original will may be held at a solicitor's office or bank, or at the Principal Probate Registry in London. It may be among the deceased person's possessions. If you do not send the original will your application will take longer to deal with.

We will not return the original will to you as it becomes a public record once it has been proved (acted on). We will, however, send you an official copy of the will with the grant of representation.

What if I don't want to apply for a grant and I am named as an executor in a will?

Executors may choose to give up all their rights to a grant ('renunciation') or they may reserve the right, ('power reserved'), to apply for a grant in the future. Unlike renunciation, power reserved will not prevent you applying for a grant at a later date should you need to do so.

Only the executor(s) who swear an oath in support of the application will be named on the grant and only their signature will be required to release the deceased person's assets.

If the person who is entitled to the grant does not wish to apply, they may appoint someone else to be their attorney to obtain the grant on their behalf. If this is the case the details of the person appointing the attorney should be entered on form **PA1**. We will then send you a form for that person to give formal authority, for you to act on their behalf. If the person entitled to the grant has already signed an Enduring Power of Attorney (EPA) or a Lasting Power of Attorney (LPA) please file the original document with your application. This document will be returned to you.

The grant will be issued in the name of the attorney but will state that it is for the "use and benefit" of the person entitled to the grant.

Note – LPA must be registered with the Office of the Public Guardian before it can be used.

You can contact them via www.justice.gov.uk/about/opg or by calling 0845 330 2900.

Why do I need to think about inheritance tax now?

The tax on the estate of a person who has died is called inheritance tax. It is dealt with by HM Revenue & Customs (HMRC). If inheritance tax is due, you normally have to pay at least some of the tax before we can issue the grant.

The issue of the grant does not mean that HMRC have agreed the final inheritance tax liability. They will usually contact you again after you have received the grant. Subject to the requirements to pay some of the tax before obtaining the grant, inheritance tax is due six months after the end of the month in which the person died. HMRC will charge interest on unpaid tax from this due date whatever the reason for late payment.

Probate registry staff are not trained to deal with queries about HMRC forms or inheritance tax. If you have any queries about these you should visit the HMRC website: www.hmrc.gov.uk/inheritancetax or contact the Probate and Inheritance Tax Helpline on 0300 123 1072.

How do I apply for a grant?

You will need to follow the process set out below:

Complete the Probate Service application form

You will need to complete **Probate Application form PA1**, using **Guidance Leaflet PA1A**. You can get these forms by:

- calling the Probate and Inheritance Tax Helpline on 0300 123 1072;
- downloading them from hmctsformfinder.justice.gov.uk. Please note, you cannot save the form online or submit electronically but you can either complete on the screen and print it, or print the blank form and complete it by hand; or
- they can be obtained by email from a probate registry.

Complete the HMRC tax form

When you apply for a grant, you will need to complete a tax form **whether or not inheritance tax is owed**. You should use form **IHT205** if no inheritance tax is payable. If form **IHT205** is not applicable to you, please contact HMRC for form **IHT400**.

For help completing the forms, you can contact the Probate and Inheritance Tax Helpline on 0300 123 1072.

Please note, no grant can issue until either it has been confirmed by you that no inheritance tax is payable, or that, if inheritance tax is payable, HMRC has confirmed to the Probate Service that the grant can issue.

Options for swearing the oath

As part of the application process you will need to swear an oath to confirm the information you have provided in the application form is true to your best knowledge and belief. The oath will also set out the legal requirements expected of you as the holder of the grant. The oath, which is a document containing all the necessary information to support the application, will be prepared for you by Probate Service staff, and you can choose to swear it either:

- at the office of any commissioner for oaths (usually a solicitor's office) convenient to yourself; or
- by attending at one of the probate venues listed in leaflet **PA4** (we will send you the oath and details of how to arrange the appointment).

Please note, it will usually take no more than five minutes to swear the oath. You may wish to take this into consideration when deciding which option you wish to take.

Before a commissioner for oaths

If you choose to go to a commissioner of oaths to swear the oath in support of your application you may be able to swear your papers closer to your home or place of work than if you attend at a probate venue. Commissioners of oaths are often solicitors but they will have no involvement either in your application or the administration of the estate; your only contact with them will be for the formal swearing of the oath – usually no more than five minutes.

The first named applicant will be sent the oath which must then be taken to a solicitor of their choice before whom they wish to swear the oath. All applicants who wish to be named on the grant will be required to swear the oath. We will send further instructions on the process to follow when we send you the oath.

A charge of £10 for each oath and 50p for each exhibit is made by the solicitor for this service. An exhibit is any document referred to in the oath and will usually be a copy of the will (if one was left). You will need to contact the solicitor to make appropriate arrangements to swear the oath. If you are outside England or Wales, different charges may apply and you may wish to check the fee beforehand and also contact the Probate Registry for further information on how to do this.

If you choose this option you should write **'solicitor's office'** in the box labelled **'interview venue'** on the first page of the form **PA1**.

This option may not be applicable in all cases and it may be necessary for you to attend an appointment at the registry. Should this apply in your case, you will be contacted by the Probate Service.

At a probate venue

If you attend a probate venue, there is no additional charge for swearing the oath, and the arrangements for you to swear the oath will be made by probate staff. The leaflet **PA4** provides more information on the locations for swearing the oath if you choose this option.

The locations highlighted in bold on the PA4 have limited opening times, as an appointment date for that venue will only be set once a minimum of 50 applications wishing to attend have been received. When selecting a venue your appointment will be fixed for the next available date. It may be that an earlier date can be given at the main registry and this will be discussed when you call.

If you choose to swear your oath at a probate venue you should write your preferred location in the box labelled **'interview venue'** on the first page of the form **PA1**.

Decide how many official sealed copies of the grant of representation you need

Organisations like banks and building societies need to see sealed copies of the grant before they can release assets to you. They won't accept unsealed photocopies.

Therefore, if you want to deal with the estate quickly, you may want to order enough sealed copies of the grant to send to all the organisations you are dealing with at the same time.

If there are any assets held outside England and Wales, those asset holders may require a copy of the grant to be provided in a different format – usually referred to as a sealed and certified copy.

It is still possible to obtain further sealed copies of the grant for official use after it has issued. You will need to write to the probate registry which issued the grant. However, these will cost more than those ordered at the time of application (see **PA3** – fees list), so it is important to decide before you apply for the grant how many copies you will need.

Make sure you enclose the correct documents

You will need to enclose:

- An official copy (**not** a photocopy) of the death certificate issued by the Registrar of Births Deaths and Marriages or a coroner's certificate.
- The **original** will and any codicils (or any document in which the deceased person expresses any wishes about the distribution of his or her estate). **Keep a copy of any will or codicil you send us**. Please do not attach anything to the will by staple, pin etc. or remove any fastenings from the will.
- Three clear and legible A4 copies of the will and any codicils.

- Any other documents specifically requested by the Probate Service or on the form **PA1**.
- The appropriate HMRC form for your application.
- A cheque made payable to 'HM Courts & Tribunals Service' for the fee, and including the cost of the number of additional copies you have requested. See the fees list on leaflet **PA3**. (We cannot process your application until the fee has been paid.)

Where should I send my application?

You should send your application to the probate registry of your choice (see leaflet **PA4** for the address). You can choose any venue for your appointment to swear the oath, **but your application must be sent to the main Probate Registry responsible for that venue**. You may wish to send your application by registered or recorded post.

Processing the application

When we receive your application, we will examine it and if we have all the information/ documentation to enable us to process your case, we will send you a letter (usually within 10-14 days of receiving your application) acknowledging receipt of your application and providing you with a copy of the oath you will need to swear.

If you have opted to swear the oath at a local solicitor you should contact that solicitor to make appropriate arrangements. We will send further instructions on the process when we send you the oath.

If you have opted to swear the oath at a probate venue, we will send the oath to you and then you can call to arrange a date convenient for you.

If you are applying for a grant with someone else and they cannot come with you, we can arrange for them to swear the oath separately at a different location if necessary. This will, however, increase the time it takes to issue your grant.

We will contact you if, after examining your application, we have any queries. If we do contact you, and you are unable to provide us with the further information and/or documentation we require, it is possible an order may be made that your application is not suitable to be dealt with as a personal application. If this is the case, you will need to instruct a solicitor or probate practitioner to make the application on your behalf.

We may require you to sign additional documents or contact other people – for example, a witness to a will – so that we can interview them or obtain their signatures on documents to help with your application.

What happens when I swear the oath?

You will be asked to sign the prepared oath and to swear, or affirm, before the commissioner of oaths or probate officer that the information you have given is true to the best of your knowledge. You will be given the opportunity to swear on the religious book of your choice.

What happens after I have sworn the oath?

If you have sworn the oath at a local solicitor, you should return it to the registry. Once we have the oath, provided we have all the necessary documentation, we will send you the original grant and copies of the grant (if you have requested them) and return the original death certificate to you, usually within seven working days. You can arrange to collect the documents in person if you want. If you wish to do this, please confirm this in a covering letter when returning the sworn oath.

We retain the original will, as it becomes a public record.

After the grant has issued

When the grant has been issued you will receive information about your role as the executor (**PA97**).

Your duties are to:

- collect the estate (money, property, etc);
- pay debts, funeral expenses etc;
- pay the balance to the persons who are legally entitled to it; and
- keep receipts and a record of what you have done.

You will have the legal right to ask any person or organisation holding the deceased person's assets to give you access to those assets. These assets can then be released, sold or transferred in accordance with the deceased person's wishes or in accordance with the law if the deceased person left no will or codicil(s).

Please note, once issued, all grants of representation, and copy wills which have been proved are public records. Copies of grants and wills can be requested by anyone, on payment of the appropriate fee (see **PA3**).

The responsibility of the Probate Service ends when the grant is issued, and we cannot advise you on how to administer the estate. If you have any questions about this, you may wish to take legal advice.

Useful contacts

For general information on wills and probate:
www.gov.uk/wills-probate-inheritance/overview

To access the online forms and leaflets:
hmctsformfinder.justice.gov.uk

To find the addresses of the regional probate registries:
courttribunalfinder.service.gov.uk/

For information about inheritance tax and online forms:
www.hmrc.gov.uk/inheritancetax

For more detailed information about probate and inheritance tax:
Probate and Inheritance Tax Helpline: 0300 123 1072

Probate forms and leaflets

PA1   Probate application form

PA1A   Probate application form
(guidance notes)

PA2   How to obtain probate (leaflet)

PA3   Probate fees list (leaflet)

PA4   Directory of probate registries and interview venues (leaflet)

PA7   How to deposit a will with the
Probate Service (leaflet)

PA7A   Withdrawing your will from the
Principal Probate Registry (form)

PA8   How to enter a caveat (leaflet)

PA8A   How to enter a caveat (form)

PA9   How to enter a general search (leaflet)

PA10   How to enter a standing search (leaflet)

PA1S   Application for a Probate Search or Standing Search (form)

HMRC Inheritance Tax forms

IHT205 Return of estate information

IHT206 Return of estate information (guidance notes)

IHT400 Inheritance Tax Account

Application for a search (copies of grants and wills)

We offer two different types of searches, General Searches and Standing Searches. Please read the following guidance to help you determine what type of search you require and then complete the details overleaf.

General Search

A search of the probate records for England and Wales from 1858 to the present day.

A General Search is suitable when searching for information about an estate or for family history research and you wish to obtain a copy of the grant and will (if any) and additionally when you do not know the exact date of death.

Standing Search

An ongoing search that anticipates the issue of a grant and entitles you to a copy of the grant and will (if any) when it issues.

Your application is entered onto a database and remains in force for 6 months. The database matches the details you have sent to us to any grant, so to ensure a correct match please ensure the accuracy of the information supplied.

The date of death of the deceased **must** be within the last **six** months and you must supply the **exact** date of death.

If the date of death is **not** within the last six months you **must** have already carried out a general search which resulted in no record being found and you need to supply a copy of your No Trace letter with this application.

A Standing Search is suitable if you need to make a claim against an estate and need to know when the grant issues.

If you submit a Standing Search application that does not meet the above mandatory criteria then we will automatically conduct a General Search as standard.

Notes

- We aim to respond to all search requests within 21 working days **(four weeks)**.

  You will be sent:

  For a **General Search** either copies or a letter explaining there is no record of a grant in the estate.

  For a **Standing Search** an acknowledgment letter to confirm your Standing Search has been entered (including a reference number should you wish to extend it for a further 6 months) or if the grant has already issued, copies of the grant and will if applicable.

- If you require a General Search urgently for a Court hearing, property sale or other legal reason, please go in person to your local Probate Registry where, if Probate has been granted, copies can usually be provided within 24 hours. Please contact the registry prior to your visit as this service is not available at all registries.

- Any queries about submitted search applications **must be made in writing** to the address below. Please only write after four weeks have elapsed confirming when payment was taken.

- For further information on searches and copies please visit our website www.justice.gov.uk

Please complete **ALL** sections on the form overleaf and send it with your payment and any supporting documents to:

The Postal Searches and Copies Department, District Probate Registry,
York House, 31 York Place, Leeds, LS1 2BA

Please complete in CAPITAL LETTERS

Details of the deceased

Surname		Alternative spelling:
Forenames		Alternative spelling:
Address		
Date of death		(must be the exact date and within the last 6 months for a Standing Search)
Probate details (if known)	Grant type:	Issuing Registry:	Date:

Type of Search requested

Please tick the appropriate box (see guidance overleaf) and only tick one box.

General Search ☐   **Standing Search** (only for deaths in the last 6 months) ☐

If no box or both boxes are ticked a general search will be undertaken by default.

Document required/payment

Standing Searches

Fee payable for a Standing Search is £10 (must meet criteria overleaf for a Standing Search to be entered).

General Searches

Fee payable for a General Search including 1 copy of the grant and 1 copy of the will is £10.
As standard the copies are **not** sealed.

For General Searches **additional** copies of the grant are £0.50 each and the will £0.50 each.

In **TOTAL**, how many copies of:

the grant do you require? ☐

the will do you require? ☐

I enclose a cheque payable to 'HMCTS' to the value of £ ☐

For General Searches, **do not** tick this box unless you require the grant to administer the estate ☐

For General Searches, if you need the copies to administer the estate abroad please state the country/countries in which the deceased held assets in the box below:

Your details

Name/organisation	
Your reference (if any)	
Your postal address or DX number (if applicable)	

Please write the name of the deceased on the reverse of the cheque. If you are sending one cheque for multiple requests, one name on the cheque is sufficient.

Index

******